Rediscovering
Christanna

REDISCOVERING CHRISTANNA

NATIVE WORLDS
AND
GOVERNOR SPOTSWOOD'S FORT

John Kincheloe

Spirit Lines Press
Alcalde, New Mexico

Rediscovering Christanna
© 2019, by John Kincheloe

All rights reserved. Neither this book nor any portion thereof may be reproduced or used in any manner whatsoever without the express written permission of the publisher, except for the use of brief quotations in a book review.

Printed in the United States of America

First Printing 2019

Print: 978-0-9831177-1-1

eBook: 978-0-9831177-2-8

Spirit Lines Press
P.O. Box 1240
Alcalde, NM 87511

Front Cover illustration © Jacob Kincheloe, 2019

Back Cover illustration © John Kincheloe, 2019

Frontispiece © John Kincheloe, 2019

johnkincheloe.contact@gmail.com

For Susan

An acceptance of English ways, however sincere, allowed them to survive in the present and gave them a long lease on the future at the cost of a certain amount of material and spiritual continuity with the past....For life is preferable to death, and those who bend to live are also possessed of courage — the courage to change and to endure in the face of overwhelming odds against their survival....

—James Axtell,
The European and the Indian

Like our economic and political worlds, stories too are defined by the principle of power. How they are told, who tells them, when they are told, how many stories are told are really dependent on power....Power is the ability not just to tell the story of another person, but to make it the definitive story of the person.... Start the story with the arrows of the Native Americans, and not with the arrival of the British, and you have an entirely different story.

—Chimamanda Ngozi Adichie,
"The Danger of a Single Story"

Yo – yágile kilé-wa yagile yónedéwahe yahahé héwa wéha wéha hé

They have carried all my relatives away, where I will never see them again.

—*Tutelo Fourth Night Spirit Release Song*

Contents

Acknowledgments i
Terminology vi
Introduction ix
The Indians' Christanna 1
"A Place of Note" 15
    The New Articles of Peace 16
    Saponie Land 21
The Fort at Christanna 25
    The Labor of Construction 27
    The Labor of Trade 33
    The Labor of Defense 39
    One Fort, Two Worlds 41
Place, Lives, and Meanings 45
    The New Town: Chunkete Posse 46
    Different Ways: Clothing and Status 53
    The Meaning of Red 61
The Idea of the Indian School 67
"A Very Handsome School" 76
    The Governor's School 77
    The Indians' School 82
Attacks on the Fort 92
Dissatisfaction and Departure 99
Persistence of Traditions 110

Two Women 119
    The Return of a Slave 122
    The Return of a Captive 124
    Storytellers 126
Understanding a Native Christanna 128
Appendix I 135
Appendix II 137
Appendix III 139
Appendix IV 141
Appendix V 143
Appendix VI 145
Appendix VII 147
Notes 149
Works Cited 183
Index 199

Acknowledgments

A special word of gratitude goes out to each librarian, archivist, digital production worker, and interlibrary loan specialist who assisted me in this project. The completion of an extensive research project requires access to many resources and the assistance of many who help make source materials available. The unsung expertise of each of these individuals was crucial to the content of this book. I am especially indebted to the staff of the Carlyle Campbell Library at Meredith College for services they provided and for their excellent collection that supported my work.

The impetus of all projects such as this one begins with curiosity. A singular role model in this aspect of the project, at the most fundamental level, is my late father who had a life-long interest in all things. Running through and about his professional and family life was a never-ending curiosity about the world. On any given day he was as likely to be reading of new developments in space exploration as archaeological findings related to the Ancient Near East. At age 100, he was intrigued by the internet and how it worked. His interest in American Indians began with his discovery of pottery shards and stone projectile points in tobacco fields when he was a boy living in eastern North Carolina. For me, that curiosity proved contagious, and I will always be grateful for his consistent example and for the life of the mind he shared with me and a great many others.

I extend my gratitude to my many friends and contacts among the three State Recognized Tribes in North Carolina who descend from the Saponie tributary Indians whose history is at the core of the Christanna story. These tribes are the Haliwa-Saponi Tribe, the Sappony, and the Occaneechi Band of the Saponi Nation. I value my interactions with people from each of these tribes, and greatly appreciate the opportunities we have had to collaborate on projects. Much of the tribal history these people share in varying degrees has been lost to time and often to historical misrepresentation. Their story of creative endurance is a powerful and important one, however, and a major goal for me in writing this book has been to tell their story well so it can be used to supplement traditions kept within their communities. My conversations with Dante Desiderio (Sappony) have been especially helpful to me over the years as I have thought about the roles indigenous people played at Fort Christanna and about how Saponie identity has evolved over time. I appreciate his thoughtful comments on an early version of the manuscript. I also received valuable responses to my manuscript from Kara Stewart (Sappony). Her comments as a teacher, a writer, and a tribal member were thought provoking and useful. Marty Richardson (Haliwa-Saponi) gave the manuscript a close reading and made good suggestions. He helped me clarify things related both to the style and the content of the book. His comments and questions encouraged me to dig deeper into the Indian understandings of events. I received additional valuable input and perspective from Lawrence Dunmore III (Occaneechi Band of the Saponi Nation). His generous responses inspired me to expand the narrative in several important places. The manuscript

Acknowledgments

is a better one as a result of the tribal responses these individuals provided. *Biláhuk*.

I extend special appreciation to those in Brunswick County, VA and elsewhere, who over many years have contributed time and resources to the effort to preserve and tell the story of Christanna by developing the Fort Christanna Historical Site. There are too many supporters of this project to name each one – hardworking individuals, members of many civic groups, contributors from the business community, and government leaders. Among those supporters, however, the members of the Board of Supervisors of Brunswick County have been salient in their vision and ongoing financial support. The members of the Fort Christanna Site Planning Committee, led by Nat Neblett, deserve applause for their commitment, tireless efforts, and perseverance in making Fort Christanna's story one that can be shared with a wide community. Their fine work to develop a historical park with interpretive signage earned a National Award of Merit in 2010 from the American Association of State and Local History, and deservedly so. It was an honor to serve as Historical Consultant on that committee for five years. In addition to Nat Neblett, several members of that Committee in particular deserve a word of special appreciation – Gay Neale, Bobby Conner, Nancy Avery, and Danny Richardson (Haliwa-Saponi). An extra measure of gratitude goes to Gay, the "Historian of Brunswick County," who with her ever-changing family of dogs generously hosted Susan and me on numerous occasions following the Christanna committee meetings. I wish I were able to extend my gratitude personally to Dorothy Thomas and to Robert "Rudy" Conner. Dorothy gave much of her time and energy to the Fort Christanna project. And Rudy, through his leadership among the County Supervisors, was instrumental in turning the vision of a public historical site into a reality. They left us too soon. The Fort Christanna Historical Site will be lasting testimony to the service of all of these fine people. Their work in telling the history of Fort Christanna to a wider public encouraged me to undertake this project.

The two primary archaeologists who worked at the Fort Christanna site deserve a special word of thanks – Mary Beaudry and Christopher Stevenson. We all owe a great debt of gratitude for their planning, field work, processing of artifacts, and accurate write ups. Their work over many years has been invaluable in clarifying and expanding our knowledge of the fort. I appreciate the very useful information they have shared with me. Chris has been especially generous in sharing his expertise and in giving me opportunities to assist in the field work he led at the Fort. I am grateful for that and for his friendship. The support of the Virginia Department of Historic Resources, the Earthwatch Institute, and the College of William and Mary has made the archaeological work at the Fort site possible, and I am deeply grateful for their timely commitment to the re-discovery of Fort Christanna.

This book would not have been even remotely possible without the unflagging support of Susan K. McClintock. It was her particular interest in the history of the Sappony tribe (of Person County, NC and Halifax County, VA) that originally opened my eyes to the need for the sort of book I have written. She has been my partner in many research adventures, my frequent editor, and my collaborator in this writing project. She

Acknowledgments

willingly took on the task of properly managing the tedious and often arcane information in the notes and bibliography. A historian by training and at heart, in the truest sense of the word, she has been my colleague in this project. Best of all, she is my friend and my wife. Throughout the project she did her utmost to protect for me the time and space the work required. My deepest and most heartfelt gratitude goes to her.

Terminology

In eighteenth-century Virginia, consistency in spelling was not given high priority. The lack of consistent spelling was even more the case when it came to non-English words and names. Consequently, tribal names were spelled in a number of ways in period documents. In order to use terms consistently and in a historically appropriate way, the most common spelling used for tribal names during the time of Fort Christanna is the spelling used in the text. The tribal names from the historical records of the period being studied are in most cases somewhat different in spelling from the modern tribal names used by Indian communities today and by some present-day scholars. Unless otherwise spelled in quotations, the names of the principal Tributary Tribes at Christanna are spelled, "Saponie," "Tottero," "Stukanocks," and "Occoneechee." Spelling variations for the other 19 tribal names mentioned in the text are sometimes noted in the text or in notes.

Tribal names are given preference in the text when references are made to Indian people. For reasons related to content or style, the terms "American Indian," "Indian," and "Native," are used interchangeably in the book to identify indigenous people of North America when needed. By intention, the term "Native American" is not used in the text. Though the term "Native American" is used heavily in government publications, in the Social Sciences, and by writers in various academic fields, it is generally less used within American Indian

Terminology

communities. Given the content of this book, the preference is to use alternate terms.

European terms for tribal leaders were imposed on Native people, and these reflected a European sense of hierarchy. Erroneous as these may be, terms such as "King" and "Queen" are used when quoted or when it seems necessary to convey a certain English understanding. Other terms, such as "Headman," "Chief Man," or "Chief" are English terms used to express the title or rank of a tribal leader. For the Saponie the title for a male tribal leader was *"Hoonskey"* or *"Hoontky."* The term for a female leader added the suffix "miha," meaning woman or wife, as in *"Hoontkymiha."* For the tribes of the Five Nations, the term commonly used to indicate a high leadership role or Paramount Chief was *"Sachem."*

Period quotations may have many grammar and spelling issues from our perspective. Only rarely has the author corrected or revised the language of the original sources. The reader is encouraged to encounter the past through the actual language and writing that was preserved from a distant and different time. For that reason a number of period quotations are presented in the text rather than summaries of them.

Until the mid-1700s in Virginia and other British territories, the beginning of the calendar year was regarded as March 25. Until that Old Style calendar was changed to our current or New Style calendar, dates from January to March 24th were regarded as being in the same calendar year of the previous nine months. For example a Virginia manuscript dated "February 27, 1713" was dated using the Old Style calendar. Using the New Style calendar today, we would regard that date as

"February 27, 1714." Understandably this can be confusing to modern readers, so in this manuscript, the year is written "February 27, 1713/14" to reflect both the original Old Style and our current New Style year.

For convenience Francis Nicholson, Alexander Spotswood, and Sir William Gooch are each referred to as "Governor" in the text, but their proper title was Lieutenant Governor. They served under the absentee Governor of Virginia, George Hamilton, 1st Earl of Orkney, who never visited the colony. While in office in Virginia a Lieutenant Governor was often referred to as "Governor."

Introduction

Most of what has been written about Fort Christanna has concentrated on aspects of its English origins and on its significance in the political and economic life of the colony of Virginia. Until very recently the historians who have given it the most attention have regarded it primarily as an aspect of Lt. Governor Alexander Spotswood's term as governor of Virginia, 1710-22.[1] The fact that Fort Christanna was a Native place as well is a narrative that has largely been ignored.

The fort's history as a Native place has remained in the shadow of Anglocentric analysis for a number of reasons. All those first writers who intentionally or inadvertently left some account of the indigenous people at Christanna were European and most were English. In eighteenth-century Virginia, Native people were regarded by those witnesses as secondary to English interests. With few exceptions, the period accounts of Native people acting within the sphere of Fort Christanna's influence are narrow in scope and culturally oriented toward European perspectives.

In addition to this, the archaeological work done at the site of the Fort yielded an assemblage that for the most part was of English or European origin. Features that were identified in the soil at the site, with few exceptions, were likewise typical of English construction and activities. Consequently, archaeologists have interpreted the Fort primarily as an English colonial fur trade center, despite a hope for discovering evidence of the changing material culture of Native people and of their cultural influence on the English who interacted with them.[2] Reinforcing an English orientation in archaeological analysis is the reality that by 1715 when Fort Christanna was completed, European goods were a major part of the lives of the indigenous people of the region. This obscures distinctly Indian identities and makes interpretation a challenge. Is the excavated English clay pipe an English or an Indian item?

The simple fact that the site of *Chunkete Posse,* the Saponie Indian town that stood near the Fort, has not been discovered means that key evidence about the people interacting in that place remains out of reach and out of our consideration. In the absence of material culture evidence from this Indian town and features it could reveal, the account of Christanna remains biased toward the English presence and goals there. One content focus in this book was developed in order to point archaeologists toward the physical site of *Chunkete Posse,* in the hope that the testimony of that lost town will help tell a balanced history of all of those who interacted at and around Fort Christanna.

Another factor obscuring the history of the Indian people at Christanna is a cultural one. In the field of American History generally, American Indian people, histories, and concerns have been marginalized, and as a result we do not look for the Indian part of the historical story. We are conditioned not to look for the Native story at Christanna when the accepted historical narrative gives only the account of "Governor Spotswood's frontier fort." Our received history misdirects by means of its Eurocentric focus, terminology, and thematic concerns.[3] In looking at

Introduction

Christanna we can't see the forest for the "Spotswoods." The Governor's portrait illustrates the published writing about the fort and its environs, and in the absence of equivalent Indian portraits or other Native images, the English slant of the Fort's history is reinforced visually. Because Alexander Spotswood's voice is the most prominent in the textual sources, the scholarly focus has been on a Christanna that is an Englishman's adventure. In this view, the notion of Spotswood's fort as a bold effort to solve English problems with Indians eclipses our consideration of how various tribes used Christanna for their own purposes and advantages.

Given the lack of balance in the primary source material, an authentic history of the Native people who interacted at Fort Christanna is a difficult thing to develop. Of necessity, the techniques required to bring into focus the Indian history at Christanna must be interdisciplinary in nature. Archaeology, ethnology, linguistics, statistics, and chemical analysis all combine with historical and ethnohistorical scholarship to recover an account of Indian lives and political intentions there. Taking advantage of the tools and perspectives of multiple disciplines, this book re-discovers a Native Christanna that has been forgotten and ignored. In re-viewing and questioning certain received versions of the historical narrative about Christanna, and through the incorporation of new archaeological findings, a very different picture of the Fort emerges.

Additional perspectives have remained in the shadow of the dominant narrative of the Fort, as well. Scholarly work on Fort Christanna has ignored women. As important as women were in Native societies, they seem all but absent in the historical sources related to the

Indians at Christanna, except as their imagined sexuality is described or suggested by certain of the English. We can't see the women's lives for the profusion of stories about men, both English and Indian. In marginalizing the lives of women who interacted at Christanna, important cultural and historical contexts have been lost. A further misdirection in our histories of the Fort derives from a modern cultural tendency to look for a unified, pan-Indian, or "Native American" story, when in reality the history of Christanna involves multiple tribes who often had tremendous cultural differences one from another, and were far from unified in their goals and methods to achieve tribal ends. The story of Christanna is both one of remarkable intertribal collaborations and one of relentless intertribal conflicts. In response to these particular deficiencies in the telling of Christanna's history, this book re-encounters the historical sources by recognizing multiple tribal perspectives and the roles, circumstances, and agency of Native women.

Understanding the Native matrix in which Fort Christanna developed brings into focus the larger picture of Southeastern Indians in the first half of the eighteenth-century. At the core of Fort Christanna's history is the story of remnant groups of several tribes that coalesced to some degree into a people the English called "Saponie." These tribal groups came together out of necessity and with the encouragement of the English. Separately, they were the major tribes – the Saponie, Tottero, Stukanocks (Stegaraki), and Occoneechee – and a less-well known tribe, the Meipontski. Later a portion of the Saraw (Cheraw) would join them. Under constant assault from Old World diseases that spared no tribes, the Indians at Christanna additionally were caught in a three-way vise.

They were relentlessly set upon from the north by militaristic bands from the Five Nations of the Iroquois Confederacy who were sometimes joined and supported by allied Iroquoian-speaking tribes in Virginia and the Carolinas. The warriors from the Five Nations (later the Six Nations), pursued their tribal interests and cultural ends through a prolonged series of attacks now often referred to as "mourning wars."[4] Records from Christanna, Williamsburg, and London reveal how these ongoing northern incursions took a constant toll on the Southern tribes culturally and demographically.

A second arm of the three-way vise came from Southeastern Indian Nations that had evolved over time into militaristic slaving societies. Warriors from these tribes preyed on smaller and otherwise vulnerable tribes, and attacked to take Indian prisoners for eventual sale as slaves to the English in exchange for European trade goods. This destructive pattern of intertribal violence, tied to the economy of the Southern slave trade and to Native dependence on European commodities, resulted in what has come to be called the Mississippian Shatter Zone – a broad region of cultural and political disruption in the Southeast in which indigenous societal structures were severely damaged or destroyed.[5] Christanna Indians were situated in Virginia at the northern edge of this Shatter Zone, and their coalescence at Christanna happened late in its manifestation, so the Saponie Tribes at the Fort were spared much of the associated violence that occurred in the Carolinas.[6] Fracture lines extending out of the Shatter Zone did have a major impact at Christanna, however, bringing both violence and many beleaguered Southern tribes to the trading fort. Slowly developing shock waves from the Shatter Zone forced many tribal groups from stressed and failing Indian polities to encounter the Saponie Tribes at Christanna as allies and competitors, and to negotiate with the English to ensure access to European trade items the tribes were dependent on.

The English were the third arm of the three-part vise that pressed in on the Indians at Christanna. From an Indian perspective, the English were the new tribe. They were a different people with a language that was even more different to those at Christanna than that of the Iroquois or the Creek. For the Indians at Christanna, the English were a powerful but ambiguous ally. The English held Native children as hostages to assure loyalty from the tribes. In exchange, the tribes gained protection and important trade advantages. The English could be suppliers of valuable goods and powerful weapons, but they also were a threat. A primary goal of the English was not only to subjugate the Saponie Tribes politically, but also to radically transform core elements of traditional culture, ranging from the traditional roles of men and women to long-held religious beliefs. Other disruptive goals of the English in Virginia involved the expansion of the colony into traditional tribal lands and the use of tribes as resources for acquiring wealth and for providing defense for the colony. The demands and policies of the English were assaultive and problematic for the Christanna Indians at many levels, but the close and persistent alliance of the Saponie Tribes with the English, the most powerful arm of the three-way vise upon them, would prove to be the key to their survival during a violent time. Their unique strategy to endure by means of a steadfast relationship with the English sets them apart from all other tribes in the region.

Introduction

A history of Fort Christanna, then, does not only deliver an account of English motives, politics, enterprise, and action in the Virginia colony. An understanding of the events surrounding the Indians that interacted at the Fort brings into focus the various cultural forces that generated the rapid and extreme transitions in Southeastern Indian polities and cultures in the first half of the eighteenth-century. The events surrounding the people at the relatively small village of *Chunkete Posse* are a lens through which we can view a larger indigenous landscape of cultural disruptions, discontinuities, pressures, assaults on tradition, and violence. At the same time, this story is an account of indigenous resourcefulness in a turbulent time, and of ways Native peoples took advantage of new opportunities for their own ends.

The telling of the story of the Indians at Christanna is not just an academic exercise. In an important way it is a giving back of this story to the communities of people who are descendants of those Christanna Indians who found ways to survive the violence of the period, the assaults on culture, and the dangerous alliances they had to make. Those Indian people are certainly the most important audience for this book. It is with a spirit of humility and responsibility that I put this history into the hands of those people who, in countless ways over centuries, have had it taken from them. I hope this book will be a useful resource alongside tribal stories they have kept related to their time at Christanna and after.

Another important audience is the reader who is curious about traditional ways of Indian people of the East and about the colonial Fort at Christanna, how it came to be, and what its purposes were. Christanna's history is a series of overlapping stories set at a cultural crossroads three hundred years ago. It is a complex Indian story, and an English one, as well. The interwoven historical narratives offer the reader a richly textured American story of power, control, diversity, violence, belief, betrayal, pathos, and endurance. My best hope is that all readers will be intrigued and informed by this account, as both a remarkable history and a remarkable story.

CHAPTER ONE

The Indians' Christanna

Neither the English nor the tribal emissaries at Fort Christanna expected what was about to happen. The Catawba party of four dozen men and women, with their children, had made camp in the woods south of the Meherrin River, about 50 yards outside the log walls of the great fort. According to the English requirements of that place, in order to maintain the peace, all those in the Indian camp had given over their weapons to be held for safekeeping by the rangers within the Fort. In the shadow of the palisade walls of Christanna, and beneath the protection of its five cannon, the Catawba awaited their long-anticipated council meeting with the Governor of Virginia.

The most important men of the powerful Catawba villages had traveled to Virginia in April of 1717 to come to the place on the Meherrin River the English called "Christanna." Lesser Headmen from allied villages had made the 250 mile journey with them. Together they had brought eleven Catawba boys, sons of the tribal leaders, just as Virginia's Governor Spotswood had instructed them. The boys were brought to be left at Christanna where they would be taught the new language English and the new Jesus religion. Their fathers and the other tribal leaders would soon return to Catawba, but these boys would remain with the hundred other children at the Indian School, where a schoolmaster, Charles Griffin, would instruct them in English ways. These boys all would be kept at Christanna as hostages, as the Governor required. This was part of his plan to ensure peace on the colony's southern frontier and fidelity to the English. The Catawba had their own reasons for bringing their children to the English fort, however. Just as it had benefitted the Saponie tribe, the Tottero, the Stukanocks, and the Occoneechee to send their children to the Indian School, the Headmen of the Catawba villages knew that co-operation with the English in this way would open a flow of trade goods that would benefit their war-damaged people.[1]

On hearing that the Catawba Headmen and others had come with their children to Christanna, Governor Spotswood hastened from Williamsburg to meet them. Sealing an agreement for peace with this powerful Western tribe would both enhance the defense of the colony's frontier and extend the lucrative fur trade that, according to regulation, passed only through Christanna to the benefit of Spotswood's Virginia Indian Company. The initial council talks on April 9, 1717 between the Catawba Headmen and Governor Spotswood went well, and the parties involved must have bedded down that night encouraged by the proceedings.

Just before dawn it happened. The quiet of the April night was split by shrill battle cries and the sharp thunder of close musket fire. Blinding flashes of hot light from flintlocks blossomed and multiplied in the near dark, spraying lead shot into the Catawba camp. Unarmed and startled from their sleep, those from the Catawba villages stumbled through the pre-dawn darkness to escape the attack, hidden only by the slow-floating blue clouds made by the gunfire. Then as suddenly as it all had begun, the war cries, the blows from war clubs, and the chaos subsided. As the acrid smoke of war was clearing, armed rangers from inside the Fort raced out to the Indian camp, but the attackers had vanished into the forest. Governor Spotswood and Rev. Hugh Jones, a fellow visitor to the Fort, would later venture out to the camp to observe what had happened. As morning light rose, the Catawba losses became clear. The Chief Man of the Catawba, *Wickmannatauchee*, was missing along with four others, including a woman. *Wickmannatauchee's* wife lay dead with four others, struck down or shot through their trade blankets. Two more lay wounded. By dawn the woods at Christanna were filled with tribal mourning songs and anger.[2]

The Catawba were livid that the English allowed the attack to happen. They accused the English of being behind the ambush. Governor Spotswood was hard pressed by the Catawba leaders, but in time he was able to convince the Headmen that the English had no part in the assault. It is a sign of the desperation of the Catawba and the need for trade goods that, even after this devastating attack, the Headmen agreed to leave their boys at the school "to be bred Christians," as the Governor had put it.[3] Hugh Jones, however, reported an important observation the Catawba leaders expressed regarding the English efforts to Europeanize them. Considering the Governor's plan to re-educate and indoctrinate the children, the leaders spoke their mind. Their interpreter reported that they "asked leave to be excused from becoming as we are, for they thought it hard, that we should desire them to change their manners and customs, since they did not desire us to turn Indians."[4]

Eleven days after the attack, one of the Catawba men taken prisoner by the pre-dawn attackers escaped from the warriors who took him. He eluded his captors and, through a feat of remarkable endurance, ran naked through the forest for days, foraging for food, eventually to make it back and report who had mounted the attack on his people. Hugh Jones, an eyewitness to the aftermath of the attack, later reported in his account of the events that the man who escaped was *Wickmannatauchee*.[5] The Catawba Headman identified the murderers as a band of "Sinequa" (Seneca), a term the Catawba and the Saponie used for the Northern Indians of the Five Nations. These were a powerful confederacy of Iroquois (*Haudenosaunee*) tribes that included the Cayuga, Oneida, Onondaga, Mohawk, as well as the Seneca. The traditional tribal homeland of the Five Nations was in the territory the English called the New York colony.

Outraged by the brazen attack at his fort, Governor Spotswood was quick to send a ranger, Christopher Smith, with an urgent letter to Governor Robert Hunter of New York, calling on him to confront the leaders of the Five Nations regarding this offensive breach of the peace, and to demand from the leaders of the Northern Tribes reparations and the release of captives taken.[6] This was not the first time Spotswood had been forced to write Hunter concerning the Five Nations incursions into

Virginia.⁷ The warfare and conflict between the Northern Iroquois tribes and those in Virginia had a long history. English leaders a generation earlier had attempted to deal with the prolonged conflict through a treaty with the Five Nations in 1685.⁸ That treaty was an attempt to deal with violence along the Warrior's Path through Virginia and with ancient intertribal conflicts that had an impact in several colonies. It seems likely the enmity was older than the colonies.⁹

In Albany on June 16, 1717, Governor Hunter met with the leaders of the Five Nations and presented Spotswood's accusations and demands. The story and the motives for the attack would slowly unfold. *Dekanissore (Teganissorens)*, the venerable Onondaga Sachem, spoke for the Five Nations in council with Hunter, and freely admitted that it was their people who had attacked the Catawba at Christanna. He identified *Aria*, a Mohawk warrior, as the leader of the attack.¹⁰

Aria and 40 warriors had developed their assault in the way that was traditional. Their tactic was to surround the enemy under cover of darkness in order to launch a surprise attack at dawn. Their stealth, the sudden assault, and rapid departure resulted in the warriors' quick success with few casualties.¹¹ William Byrd II described at some length the military strategy of the Northern Indians in his *History of the Dividing Line* (1728). If those tribes should discover a camp of Southern Indians, he wrote, "they Squat down in some Thicket, and keep themselves hush and Snug till it is dark; Then creeping up Softly, they approach near enough to observe all the Motions of the Enemy. And about two a clock in the Morning, when they conceive them to be in a Profound Sleep, for they never keep Watch and Ward, pour in a

Volley upon them, each singling out his Man. The Moment they have discharg'd their pieces, they rush in with their Tomahawks, and make sure work of all that are disabled.... Sometimes, when they find the Enemy Asleep around their little Fire, they first Pelt them with little Stones to wake them, and when they get up, fire in upon them, being in that Posture a better Mark than when prostrate on the Ground."[12] It was an approach to warfare shared by many tribes. Hugh Jones had seen similar tactics in use among the Virginia tribes: "They attack always by surprise, and will never stand their Ground when discovered; but will fly to Ambush, whither the Enemy may pursue with Peril of his Life."[13]

The aggression at Fort Christanna was not a random event. It was part of a never-ending war of reciprocal vengeance that arose out of a complex mixture of tribal kinship responsibilities and a sense of religious duty. When a life was taken, retaliation in kind was thought to be necessary to restore balance, and in some cases to provide satisfaction for the souls of those who were killed.[14] The moral code of all the Indian peoples acting within the sphere of Christanna's influence was everywhere the same: a wrong done to one's family, one's clan, or one's village must be avenged by an equivalent act on those who perpetrated the offence. For the Northern Indians, for the Catawba and their allies, and for the Saponie Tribes at Christanna, alike, it was proper and expected that wrongs against them would be avenged by a like offence to the perpetrators. But for the Northern Iroquois, revenge attacks additionally involved the motive of taking prisoners who, if not ritually executed, might be incorporated ceremonially into a clan to replace individuals who were lost to disease or warfare.[15] Bereaved women encouraged bands of young Iroquois warriors to wipe away their grief by going out to fight tribal enemies, and to return with prisoners. Following a raid, the prisoners were distributed among the bereaved women. The women then decided the fate of the captured individual — either an incorporation into the clan and family to replenish a particular tribal loss, or a fate of protracted torture, led by elder women, and eventual execution. Understood in this context, the attack on the Catawba by *Aria* and his raiding party was motivated in part by a culturally defined tribal grieving process.[16]

Beyond those motives, such attacks were encouraged by a tribal culture in which a young man attained status and prestige through pursuit of the warrior ideal. Hugh Jones knew that the attack at Christanna was a rite of passage for many Iroquois warriors. He wrote, "They report that the Northern Indians send out Bodies of young Fellows yearly, who dare not return without a certain Number of Scalps or Prisoners, in order to train them up, and qualify them for great and fighting men."[17] Success or failure in warfare, and the ability to form a war party could determine many things for a young Iroquoian warrior, including his ranking within his clan and village, his prospects for a prestigious marriage, and his potential for leadership opportunities.[18] Additional societal expectations of the warrior determined even the tactical approach of *Aria*'s raiding party. The Iroquois had an aversion to casualties and loss of life that was consistent with the concern to maintain tribal population. The greatest success in battle for *Aria* would come with capturing prisoners and suffering no losses. The pre-dawn, surprise attack of the Mohawk on the Catawba should be understood in part as a warrior's tactic, chosen in response to the larger expectations of his society.[19] So for the Iroquoian war party, their attack was a multivalent action that involved a complex set of interwoven motives deeply rooted in the culture of Iroquoia.

Through his questioning of the Sachem of the Five Nations on June 17, 1717, Governor Hunter would uncover a particular reason for the surprise attack at Christanna. The Sachem *Dekanissore* first denied an accusation that the escaped prisoner had asserted, namely that the Saponie were the intended victims. Then he made clear the real reason for the attack of *Aria* and his war party. *Dekanissore's* words were spoken in the Iroquois language and translated into English that was entered in this way into the record of the council:

> "Those Indians called by the English Cattawbaws are called by us Toderichroone, are a false & treacherous people; we have twice had sad experience of it. Our people had concluded a firm peace and alliance with them three years ago, and were in companie together, but the said Indians rose up in the night time while the Indians of the Five Nations were asleep and kill'd four of them and wounded one in the shoulder, who dy'd last summer. This perfidious murder they acted the same night after they had concluded the peace: the people that were thus murder'd by them belonged to the Cayouges [Cayougas] one of our Five Nations.
>
> "The Indians in those parts [Cattawbaw tribes] have been a long time our enemies...
>
> "We have now told you the reason why our people have don(e) this deed, because they so treacherously murder'd our people...."[20]

The Indians' Christanna

So the attack at Christanna was not about the English presence in the region. In fact the English and their powerful cannon were ignored in the assault. It was not about competing territorial claims. It was not about the trade in pelts and the important role Christanna and many tribes had in relation to that. For the people of the Five Nations, the Mohawk assault on April 10 was fundamentally a moral act to satisfy the wrong done by the Catawba to the Cayuga.

The year before this attack, it was the Saponie who wanted reciprocal vengeance on their enemy. John Fontaine, a visitor at Fort Christanna, wrote in his journal that twelve Headmen of the Saponie, a tribe "always at peace with the English," came to Governor Spotswood on April 15, 1716, shortly after the Governor had arrived at the Fort.[21] They gave their benefactor a gift of pelts and ceremoniously affirmed their allegiance to the English. Then the main Saponie spokesman told of a recent ambush by "Genitos" that left 15 Saponie hunters dead.[22] The Saponie Headman (or Hoonskey) asked their great ally, Governor Spotswood, to join them in a war to kill an equal number of them. The Governor refused to join their fight of revenge, but agreed to provide the Saponie with powder and shot so they could avenge the wrong. In so doing, the Governor had edged into a moral universe that was very different from his own. Spotswood became a part of the ancient blood feuds between the Five Nations tribes and the Southern tribes, feuds that had extended across Indian country for generations and must have pre-dated the arrival of the English.

The colonies struggled with the ongoing tribal wars of revenge, and most prominently attempted to deal with them later in the Treaty of Albany in 1722, and the

Council of 1744. Those talks would draw in colonial governors and representatives from the colonies of New York, Pennsylvania, Maryland, and Virginia. [23]

The events of April 15, 1716 and April 10, 1717 were more than simply an Indian ambush and an early morning attack at an English fort. To understand fully the significance of these two historical events at Fort Christanna, we need to understand their Indian contexts. The events, comprehended fully, are glimpses into a set of tribal realities we might call the Indians' Christanna. Hidden beneath and within the details in the English historical records that describe events at Christanna lie moral, cultural, and civic meanings that are distinctly Indian and very different from those comprehended by Europeans. In some sources the Native details are explicit, and in others important content is inadvertent or only hinted at.

A close reading of the details of Fontaine's April 15, 1716 account of the Saponie response to the Genito attack reveals additional aspects of a distinctly Indian Christanna. Details of his account bear repeating with a somewhat different focus: Headmen of the Saponie came to Fort Christanna to meet Governor Spotswood on April 15, 1716. They gave him a gift of pelts and, though some among them could speak English, they asked the Governor for an interpreter. Interpreters were used by Southeastern tribes and chiefdoms at the most important meetings with the English. The use of an interpreter was an important part of Indian diplomacy, as the involvement of a trusted and experienced language expert ensured a clear exchange of meanings for the parties involved. Interpreters were familiar with the rhetorical style and metaphorical language of Native speechmakers, and with the cultural contexts – Indian and English – of what was being spoken.[24] Beyond this, though, from a Saponie perspective the call for the interpreter was more than simply the need for a translator. For the Native men involved, the request for an interpreter was a coded aspect of the tribal ritual of diplomacy with the English. For the Saponie the tribal call for an interpreter signified that this was to be a meeting of the highest order of importance. Fontaine, the French adventurer, seems to have been completely unaware of the tribal meaning of the Saponie request. English leaders in Virginia, however, were aware to some degree of the importance of the interpreter as a cultural go-between. Interpreters such as William and Charles Kimball, were employed through the House of Burgesses and Council as late as 1729 to assist in diplomatic meetings with the Saponie and Occoneechee.[25]

Just as the request for an interpreter was part of the Saponie ritual of diplomacy, so too was the Headmen's gift of pelts to the Governor. For the Saponie, as it was for other eastern tribes, the offering of gifts during important diplomatic talks was a time-honored, ritualized act done to ensure reciprocity, build an alliances, maintain stability in relationships, and achieve success.[26] Though by the first part of the eighteenth-century the Native pattern of gift giving was beginning to evolve into a new and European-influenced pattern of commodity exchange, the traditional use of gifts in diplomatic meetings persisted, as this 1716 meeting at Christanna shows. Fontaine likely understood the gift to be simply an act of fealty or obeisance, but for the Saponie Headmen, the gift of pelts was part of the tradition of indigenous diplomacy, an act calculated to reinforce and manipulate the political relationship with Spotswood. Giving such a gift was a powerful way for the tribal representatives to assert their political and spiritual authority and to leverage the request that would follow.

Fontaine inadvertently noted still another kind of indigenous symbolic act in their meeting with Spotswood. Fontaine wrote in his journal, "So the Governor got an interpreter, after which they stood silent for a while, and after they had spit several times upon the ground one of them began to speak...." For the Governor and the European writer of the journal, the spitting likely seemed merely uncouth, bucolic, or insignificant. For the Saponie Headmen, however, the observed act of spitting may have had ceremonial meaning associated with tribal traditions. Two interpretations based on Southeastern Indian ethnographic knowledge support this understanding.

Throughout the Southeast for generations it was common for Native men to cleanse or purify themselves before the most important tribal events – before warfare, before spiritually important ceremonial games, and before council meetings between the representatives of chiefdoms. For the Southeastern tribes acts of ritual cleansing took many forms.[27] It sometimes involved the communal use of potions made from button snakeroot or yaupon holly. Drinking tea made from these plants would result in a vomiting that was understood to cleanse the body and clear the mind. Rev. Hugh Jones reported that, while at Christanna, he witnessed what must have been this type of purification at a funeral ceremony. He wrote of the Indians' "howling Lamentations and Purgation at their Burials."[28] So John Fontaine's written observation about the Saponie time of silence followed by spitting may be an unwitting documentation of a symbolic act of purification – perhaps a devolved one – akin to other such ceremonial traditions of purification that, for many regional tribes and at Christanna, preceded the highest-level tribal events.

 Another interpretation is suggested in the writing of John Lawson, the English explorer and Surveyor, who observed spitting as a sacred ceremonial act in his travels in 1701 among tribes to the south that were related to the Saponie. Lawson wrote in his *New Voyage to Carolina*: "The next day, we went over several Tracts of rich Land, but mix'd with Pines and other indifferent Soil. In our way, there stood a great Stone about the Size of a large Oven, and hollow; this the Indians took great Notice of, putting some Tobacco into the Concavity, and spitting after it. I ask'd them the Reason of their so doing, but they made me no Answer." [29] In this act, we see again the connection of spitting with ceremony. Rather than being simply a random and meaningless act, the spitting Lawson observed was, for his Eno, Shakori, and Adshusheer guides, a religious act associated with a belief held at several towns. The spitting was part of a ceremonial act that had an unspoken spiritual importance. This may further reveal a Native significance to the silence and spitting that Fontaine observed fifteen years later.

On April 15, 1716, then, the twelve Saponie Headmen came in a solemn way to meet with the leader of the English. In presenting an honor gift of pelts, in calling for an interpreter, and by performing certain acts that appear to have been part of a ceremonial formula, they introduced important traditional cultural signifiers into their meeting with the Governor. For the Saponie

Headmen these elements defined the extreme importance of the meeting, and through them they asserted their authority. These acts were culture-specific signifiers, however, and their tribal meanings apparently were mostly lost on their European counterparts. For John Fontaine, the Native leaders simply gave the Governor a gift of hides; they requested a translator when they didn't actually need one; the Saponie men just spat on the ground. As we look carefully at small details in Fontaine's account of the meeting at Fort Christanna, we discover a larger but hidden Native narrative. The Saponie Headmen came to the Fort empowered by their traditions. They met Virginia's Governor, and their intention was to manipulate him through the rituals of indigenous diplomacy.

CHAPTER TWO

"A Place of Note"

It is no coincidence that the April attacks of 1716 and 1717 happened near Governor Spotswood's great Fort at Christanna. The Saponie Indians who were attacked by the Genito were the tribe that was most engaged in the activities of the Fort, and they were the Governor's most favored Nation. The Saponie were the first to bring their children to the Indian School. The tribe remained at the Fort longer than any other Indians, and even longer than the English. As for the Catawba (Cattawbaw, Catawber), like many other Carolina and Virginia tribes, they regarded the Fort at Christanna as a preferred place for council talks with the Governor, who over time met with representatives of more than 20 tribes there. The Fort was a favored place for the Catawba to advance tribal initiatives, in part because it was situated in Indian country and closer to their villages than Williamsburg. For those reasons the Catawba were willing to deliver eleven children to the place to join those of the Saponie at the Christanna School. Beyond this, for all the tribes of the Carolina and Virginia Piedmont, the Fort was for a time both the central point of exchange in their fur trade with the English and their primary source for European trade goods – fire-arms, gunpowder and lead shot, metal knives and pots, colored English blankets, and more.

But what was the initial purpose of this fort for the English, and how did it come to be built in 1714 where it was – at the extreme edge of English influence in Virginia?

The New Articles of Peace

In 1713 Governor Spotswood and the Virginia colony were beset with difficulties. An unsettling Indian war was raging to the south. Virginia colonists were alarmed at the scope and violence of the Indian war in Carolina that had begun in the fall of 1711, and threatened the southern borderlands. The Lower Tuscarora, an Iroqouian-speaking group led by Chief Hancock, attacked colonial settlements by surprise and in a systematic way. In response to the impact of European diseases on their population, to expanding colonial encroachment on their lands, to abuses by English traders, and to enslavement by the English, Hancock's forces unleashed their fury on the North Carolina colonists. Tuscarora assaults even approached the colonial seats of power. Baron von Graffenried, the leader of the Swiss and German Palatine settlement in Bath County, was captured by the Tuscarora and later released. His companion, John Lawson, explorer and Surveyor General of North Carolina, was executed by them.[1] Many other Indian nations and tribal confederacies in addition to the Tuscarora were drawn into the protracted conflict, including the Yamasee, Cherokee, and Catawba. As the war developed, Virginia joined North and South Carolina in the war to the south.

In addition to the problems in Carolina, Virginia had Indian conflicts within its own boundaries. In 1713 alone, by the Governor's reckoning, more than 20 colonists had been killed or "carried off" by Indians. Mistreatment of Indians by unscrupulous colonial traders provoked tribes to anger.[2] The expanding English population spread into traditional lands used by tribes in the east and in the Piedmont, and differing lifeways precipitated conflicts and violence. The longstanding wars of retaliation between various tribes further upset the peace and often were misinterpreted by colonists, resulting in problems that ranged from misguided policies to loss of life. Cultural clashes were frequent at this time in Virginia when various human spaces and belief systems were colliding – clashes between tribes, many of which differed greatly one from another, and clashes between Indians and colonials.

Virginia's Governor confronted these challenges with a comprehensive solution, from his perspective. On February 27, 1713/14, Spotswood completed new treaties with three separate tribal groups — the Siouan-speaking Saponie, Occoneechee, Tottero, and Stukanocks; the Iroquoian-speaking Nottoway and Meherrin; and the Northern faction of the Tuscarora, also Iroquoian-speaking.[3] At the same time the Governor successfully advanced his "Act for the Better Regulation of the Indian Trade."[4] In the three treaties, Spotswood drew on principles that had been laid out more than a generation earlier in the important treaty, the 1677 "Articles of Peace" at Middle Plantation. That treaty and a still earlier Treaty of 1646 had established boundary lines around Indian lands and, against the pressure of English expansion, entitled tribes to possession and use of Indian land.[5] [Appendix 1] The Treaty of Middle Plantation had promised the signatory tribes a certain measure of protection, and it also set out the requirements for tribes to gain favorable "tributary status." Through a symbolic annual tribute of three arrows to Virginia's Governor, the so-called "Tributary Indians" acknowledged submission to the English and in return received benefits for being an ally to the colony.[6]

Spotswood hoped to accomplish many things through the new treaties of 1713/14. They reaffirmed the Treaty of Middle Plantation and the principle of "tributary status" for Indians co-operative with the English, requiring a tribute of only three arrows annually. The new treaties engaged the Tributary Tribes in assisting with the defense of the colony's southern border and in responding to the incursions of foreign tribes. This promised the government a reduction in expenses, as the colonial militia would shrink from 11 troops of 12 men each to a total force of only 24 men.[7] Furthermore the treaties promised protected land for the tribes. The language in the treaty made it clear that this land would be useful for both the defense of the colony and the protection of the Tributary Tribes.

> And it being found that the too near scituation (sic) of the said Indians to the other inhabitants doth occasion frequent disputes and controversies between them and is also inconvenient for the hunting by which the Said Indians alone subsist, Whereupon the aforesaid Governour of Virginia being desirous to remove the said inconveniencies, and to settle the said Indians in a manner more serviceable for the security of the Inhabitants of

> Virginia, and more beneficial to the Indians themselves...[articles of the treaty follow]

The related "Act for the Better Regulation of the Indian Trade" dealt with irregularities and conflicts in the Indian trade by the creation of the Virginia Indian Company.[8] As envisioned, this company funded by stockholders would be the sole conduit for all furs exchanged in the important peltry trade south of the James River. Thus it would eliminate abuses in the exchange of trade goods and would provide a mechanism for affording the most beneficial rates of exchange to the Tributary Tribes. To ready the colony for defense, the company was required to contribute toward the upgrading the public Magazine in Williamsburg and refreshing the stores of powder there. The company, as well, had the responsibility of funding the construction of a frontier fort on the Indians' land. Tied to Spotswood's larger conception of the fort, both the Act and the *Treaty* laid the groundwork for a plan to Christianize and re-educate the Tributaries according to English values.[9]

In the end only the Siouan-speaking tribes fully complied with the new treaty.[10] The representatives of those tribes signed the Treaty of 1713/14, endorsing their tribal responsibilities and claiming their rights as Tributaries. Their names are listed on the treaty: *Tawhee Sockha* Hoontky (or Headman) of the Saponie Indians, *Nehawroose* in behalf of the Hoontkymiha (or Headwoman) of the Stukanoe Indians, *Chaweo* in behalf of the Hoontky of the Occoneechee Indians, and *Mawseeuntkey*, Hoontky of the Tottero Indians. In a letter to the Bishop of London, Spotswood described these tribes as "a people speaking much the same language, and therefore confederated together, tho' still preserving their different Rules." The Governor soon came to refer to all of these tribes collectively as "Saponie."[11] [Appendix II]

English intentions in the Treaty are spelled out clearly in its language, but how did the Saponie Tributaries regard this treaty, and what were their intentions in this interaction? Signing a document was an act that was in its essence something alien to the tribes Spotswood called Saponie. The signatories had no cultural context for doing such a thing or for understanding a treaty as a political instrument. Though some of the tribal representatives may have recalled accounts of a similar ceremony with the English a generation earlier (the Treaty of Middle Plantation), the signing of a written treaty was a kind of ceremony without roots in their tribal culture. For the Indians involved, it is not likely that the Treaty itself was central to the meeting. The document was something scratched onto rectilinear skins with straight edges, and its content was many words in a foreign language. Because the Saponie held feathers in high regard, the English use of a feather quill at the signing may have summoned greater significance for the document than it might otherwise have had.

Given the importance of political gift giving in Native diplomacy, what the Governor regarded as a quit-rent or tribute of three arrows would be understood very differently by the tribal representatives. From an indigenous perspective, the annual gifting of three arrows is best understood as something the Saponie Tribes chose to do to secure the relationship between governments, and to assert their authority in the traditional way — through the power of the diplomatic gift. There likely was tribal memory of the earlier regular gifting of three arrows associated with the terms of the Treaty of Middle Plantation. For the representatives of the Tributary Tribes, the gift of three arrows was surely a more important political act than making their marks on the document the English called a "treaty."

The treaty talk with the Governor was certainly mediated by an interpreter who made clear the requirements and terms. The text of the treaty does not give an account of tribal response or a sense of any negotiation. The meeting must have been largely a one-way conversation, as all of the text was set in place. The reading and interpretation of the treaty addressed important tribal issues, however, in a way that must have been heard with favor. Those who cheated the tribe in trade would be dealt with. Land free from English encroachment would be theirs. The representatives must have heard through the interpreter that they would benefit in the deerskin trade from advantageous rates of exchange. Their warriors would fight together with English warriors as allies. And beyond what was written on the skins, they must have understood that the relationship they were building would secure for them a powerful military protector and reliable access to firearms, powder and shot, and other valuable trade goods. As different and dangerous as the men with wigs may have been, the gift of three arrows to the Governor must have seemed a good strategic thing to do.

Saponie Land

In the fall of 1714, Virginia's Governor Spotswood undertook a six-week journey to identify possible locations for forts.[12] The 36 square mile tract of land was selected and surveyed. The land for the Saponie Tribes was a great square that sprawled across both sides of the Meherrin River in what later would become Brunswick County, close to the location of present-day Lawrenceville, Virginia and near the intersection of State Routes 58 and 46. More than twenty Brunswick County land patents and deeds from 1724-1786 reference the "Indian line." [Appendix III] Below are citations that mark where the eastern and western boundary lines cross the Meherrin River:

> Virginia Patent Book 12:111, 23 Oct 1724. Nathaniel Harrison. 4245 acres" Beginning on the side of the said River where the Lower Line [i.e., farthest downriver] of the Sappony Indian's land crosses it, thence by the Indian's Line North..."
>
> Virginia Patent Book 13:59, 31 Oct 1726. George Hix, Jr. 429 acres" North East Ninety Nine poles to the Indian Line thence North along the same Ninety Six poles to a Walnut Tree on the River...."

Common knowledge of the boundaries of the Saponie land has long faded away, but a survey of period land grants, deeds, and the related patchwork of plots reveals clearly its outline. The tract was a geometrically perfect square that measured six miles on each side; its neat boundary lines ran exactly north-south and east-west. [Appendix IV]

This tract of land was set aside for the use of the Saponie, Occoneechee, Stukanocks, and Tottero through the treaty with "the honorable Alexander Spotswood Her Majesty's Lieutenant Governor and Commander in Chief of the Colony and Dominion of Virginia, for and in behalf of her Majesties said Colony." Hunting land was identified for the Tributaries, with a division between that set aside for the Saponie Tribes and that set aside for the Nottoway. Should advancing English settlement encroach on the tract, the Treaty stipulated that a similar tract was to be provided for them at a safe distance from the settlers, and compensation was promised for improvements left behind. In the event of a loss in population to an "inconsiderable" number, the Treaty promised 100 acres per person and access to hunting land.

This thirty-six square mile tract has often been referred to as a "reservation," but that term is never used in the *Treaty* or in other documents from the period. The term "reservation," as a description of land set aside by a government for occupation by American Indians, was not used until 1789. Our sense of that word today has unavoidable connotations of the reservations established during the 19th century period of Indian wars in the west, where defeated Indians were confined by the military. The Saponie Tribes were not militarily defeated by the English, however. They were tribes who in 1714 were allied with the English as tributaries. In 1729 when the Saponie Tribes relocated to Carolina, the English were fully aware of the move and offered no resistance.[13]

For the colonial government in Virginia, tracts of land set aside for Indians, such as those marked off for the Saponie, and earlier for the Chiskiak, Gingaskin, Mattaponi, Meherrin, Pamunkey, and Wiccocomico, served to isolate tribes from encroaching colonial settlement. Geographical segregation of the tribes through the designation of certain tracts as exclusively Indian land was an English mechanism for curtailing abuses of Indians at the hands of traders and settlers, mistreatment that often resulted in violent conflicts. For the Indian tribes involved, such tracts were important in a number of ways. They set precedents for Indian-

English governmental relations. By means of such tracts, the tribes claimed a clearly defined land base, legal protection for it, and a certain independence from the new dominant culture. To a certain degree, the tracts were an affirmation of tribal sovereignty during a time when tribal identities were under assault. And importantly, these protected land bases were places where, during a turbulent time, confederacies of surviving tribal groups forged new Indian identities.

CHAPTER THREE

The Fort at Christanna

The large Fort that Governor Spotswood conceived and laid out stood in the geographical center of the Saponie land tract at a commanding location on a hill above the Meherrin River. The Fort was a major part of Spotswood's idea for Christanna – it was mentioned seven times in three articles of the Treaty of 1713/14. He would later write, "It was in Aug'st 1714, that I began to build the fort of Christanna, and to form a Scheme for the better defending the frontier."[1] The fort was completed in the following year. But as early as January of 1715 he already was already informing the Bishop of London that, "...By the Temptation of a fine Tract of Land of Six Miles Square, the building a Fort thereon and placing a Guard of Twelve men and an Officer to be assisting to them, I engaged the Saponie, Oconeechee, Stuckanox and Tottero Indians...imediately to remove to y't place, which I have named Christ-Anna."[2] It was a name that surely would have pleased both his Anglican and royal supporters, as it was a nod both to his Saviour and his

Sovereign, Queen Anne, who died in London just as work at Christanna was begun.

In its day Fort Christanna was a grand frontier project. Pentagonal in design, the Fort's five sides enclosed nearly three-and-a-half acres. Its log walls protected numerous buildings within that were used in support of the fur trading enterprise. Five 1400-pound cannon were situated there, positioned to defend against Indian encroachment.[3] The earliest records of the details of the Fort's outer dimensions come from the travel journal of John Fontaine, who in 1716 visited Christanna with Governor Spotswood. "It is an inclosure of five sides," Fontaine wrote, "made only with pallisadoes, and instead of five bastions, there are five houses which defend the one the other – each side is about one hundred yards long."[4] Modern archaeology corroborates Fontaine's general estimate of the length of the palisade walls. His figure only overestimated the length of the walls by about 3.5 meters.[5] Excavation has further confirmed that, in fact, wooden houses did serve as defensive bastions at each of the Fort's five corners. Archaeological investigation has also revealed an additional feature of the Fort's outer structure – a catwalk that rimmed at least part of the interior of the walls.[6]

In the standard descriptions of Fort Christanna, we encounter, then, a marvel of English initiative and design. But a detailed consideration of the actual work done at and through the Fort reveals that Native involvement was a critical and likely primary factor in the successes of all the primary enterprises undertaken at Fort Christanna.

The Labor of Construction

An understanding of the labor required to complete a project of this scale points us to the identity of Spotswood's workers, a fact that was not documented at the time, but one that is important for understanding Indian involvement at the Fort. Whatever else one might say about a fort of this size and with these defensive features, it is important to think about the amount of wood involved in the enterprise and the labor required to fell and to split that timber into usable material. A letter to Richard Beresford in 1716 described the Fort's "log-houses which serve for bastions, and a curtain of mauld wood with earth on the inside from one house to another, etc. Each house has a great gun about 1400 lb."[7] Archaeological excavation has confirmed the construction, materials, and details described in the letter and in Fontaine's *Journal*.[8] Understanding that each wall of the Fort was a 12 foot high curtain of logs set side-by-side into a trench that ran for nearly 300 feet, we can make a good estimate of how many trees the palisade alone required. Archaeological evidence related to the Fort's construction indicates that workers felled trees around 6" in diameter, stripped them of branches, cut them into lengths of around 14 feet, then using wedge and maul, split them lengthwise for eventual incorporation into the walls. The logs were transported some distance to their destination on the rising ground above the river. It is reasonable to think that construction of the Fort's palisade required around 1500 split wall-logs.

Structures within the Fort required an additional quantity of lumber. We know of five substantial bastion houses, a defensive interior catwalk, and storage and livestock buildings that each required wood for construction.⁹ A trading fort required a sturdy structure to house the goods to be traded to the tribes, and a secure place to hold the pelts and skins that were received for processing and delivery east. There is no description of such a structure at Fort Christanna, but the trading cabin there must have been a log house similar to the one described in a South Carolina letter to a Capt. Glover, Aug 9, 1716. A portion of the letter describes a Store House, "...to be built within the Body of the Fort, (and a small trading Room or House in some of the Outworks of the same, for conveniency of Trading, intirely under the Command of the Fort)...Let the Houses be strong built and commodiously contrived and tight."[10] In addition, the Christanna School-Master Charles Griffin wrote to London of a "very handsome" Indian schoolhouse. There is archaeological evidence of a forge at the Fort site, and this is consistent, again, with contemporaneous observations recorded in the 1716 letter to Beresford: "I saw abundance of iron, steel and other utinsils carrying thither, there is a couple of forges sett up, and it is expected it will be a place of note."[11] Beyond all of the wood required for construction, the users of the Fort required wood for winter heating and for cooking throughout the year. An imagined Christanna Fort, then, was a large structure situated on a hill that was practically deforested. This was not only of strategic value for a frontier fort. It was the inevitable result of the expansive plan of the fort.

Given the great quantity of material used in the Fort's construction and operation, the question of labor arises. The documentary evidence from the period does not provide a complete account of Spotswood's labor force.

Who was it that felled that number of trees with hand axes, stripped, cut, and split the lumber with mallets and wedges, and hauled it to the location where the Fort and its interior buildings were being constructed? Who dug the trenches into which the wall-logs were set vertically? Who provided the labor for the various buildings of the Governor's expansive frontier enterprise? The Governor's correspondence indicates that the Fort was begun in August, 1714, and that the Fort was fairly complete by the end of March, 1715.[12] Who on the Virginia frontier was available to build this fort in just over seven months, some being winter months? There are but a few possible answers.

John Fontaine mentions in his 1716 journal the rangers at Christanna: "There are twelve men continually here to keep the place."[13] These men, their officer Capt. Robert Hix, and the School-Master were the only English permanently assigned to the Fort. According to the terms of the Treaty of 1713/14, the rangers and their officer were stationed at the Fort to defend the Virginia frontier and to supervise the movement of the Tributary Indians. A 1716 letter from Spotswood indicates that, on occasion, some rangers would be away from the Fort on patrol. He wrote: "Twelve white Men and an Officer, who were designed to be employed to Range, two or three of them at a time, with ten or twelve Indians, and in times of danger frequently to beat the Woods between Settlement and Settlement."[14] Perhaps these Rangers were the labor force who, in addition to protecting the frontier, and taking care of day-to-day needs, built the Fort in seven months through the fall and into winter. This does not seem likely.

Did Robert Hix have other resources to build Christanna? Did the Governor somehow provide the labor needed to construct the Fort? Were slaves brought in as the labor force? If so, there is no record for any of this. A partial answer comes from patent records. Fourteen small land patents were given to several men, "in consideration of divers services performed towards making a new settlement for the Saponie Indians at Christanna, pursuant to a Treaty with that Nation."[15] They must have assisted in the clearing of new roads and in hauling wagons loaded with food, powder and lead shot, firearms, tools, nails, window glass, storage barrels, and trade items. Osteoarchaeological analysis of bones excavated at the fort site tells us that livestock was brought there in substantial numbers – cattle, pigs, and goats or sheep.[16] Each of the five 1400-pound cannon with its carriage had to be transported, as well, from Williamsburg, a distance of around 100 miles. There is no doubt that the "divers services performed" by these men were demanding. But, beyond these 14 men, no additional laborers are documented. It is difficult to explain from period documents alone the labor force that acquired, processed and transported the volume of timber required to build Christanna's expansive fort and its interior buildings.

An obvious answer does present itself, however. The Indian presence in and around the Fort is well-documented throughout its history. The Indians known to have the greatest presence at Christanna, the Saponie Tribes, were not enemies of the colony. On the contrary, they were Tributary Indians who had signed the Treaty of Middle Plantation (1677) and the Treaty of 1713/14 with representatives of the King of England.[17] The history of the period reveals these tribes as consistent allies of the English and involved with colonial trade. They even built a town for themselves in close proximity to the Fort. In considering the question of the labor required to build and maintain the Fort, we are guided by to the wisdom of Occam's razor: when several explanations are available, the simplest is preferred. The labor force is simply difficult to explain without considering the probability of Indian assistance. It is only reasonable to think that the Siouan Tributary Tribes – the Indians Spotswood thought most highly of and whose presence at the Fort was most considerable – that the Saponie Tribes themselves were part of the labor force behind the construction of Christanna.

The Governor wrote in his January 27, 1714/15 letter to the Bishop of London that the Saponie, Occoneechee, Stukanocks, and Tottero had already relocated to Christanna.[18] The tribes, then, were at Christanna during the time of the Fort's construction. It makes sense that the Governor would have engaged the Tributary Tribes in this project, just as he engaged them as partners in the fur trade and in the defense of the colony. Beyond speculation, it is well documented that the practice of involving trading tribes in the construction of colonial trading centers was common in Carolina and Georgia at that time.[19] In discussing this, archaeologist Carol I. Mason summarizes: "When European trade was first extended to any one [Indian] town, the people were apparently expected to provide sufficient labor for constructing the trading house and warehouse and also for keeping these buildings in repair. Desire for trade in the towns was enough motivation to organize them for this type of labor...."[20] It is unlikely that the savvy Governor Spotswood was unaware of this practice. And given the complex network of intertribal communication that extended over great distances, it is equally unlikely that the Saponie Tribes were unaware of this opportunity for them.

John Fontaine's journal gives us an additional detail that in a small way supports this conclusion. On April 17, 1716, Fontaine left the confines of Fort Christanna to visit the "Saponey Indian town" where the Tributaries resided. The Saponie had relocated after 1713 and had built a town down the hill "within musket shot" of the Fort.[21] He observed the Saponie town carefully and noted in his journal that "the walls of their houses are large pieces of timber, which are squared." The squaring of timbers is a building technique that has clear European origins. It leads us to the conclusion that this non-Indian technique of construction may have been learned during their assistance with the construction of buildings at Fort Christanna. Fontaine's small detail, then, lends further support to the idea that the Fort was constructed with Tributary Indian labor.

The evidence for the use of Indian labor in the construction of Fort Christanna is circumstantial, as records from the period shed only a little light on the subject. In light of the larger picture of relations between the Saponie and the colony, however, this understanding makes good sense. Why, after all, should Governor Spotswood not have wanted to use Tributary Indian labor? It was a resource already on hand in the westernmost part of the colony. It was labor that would come reasonably with the exchange of inexpensive European goods. In fact, the Treaty of 1713/14 reveals that it was Spotswood's original intention that the Indians would build the Fort. Articles V and VI entitle the tribes to incorporate into one Nation on their land "whereon they may build a Fort." The rangers and an officer were assigned "to reside at their Fort" to defend their settlement.

The Treaty of 1713/14 was not only the Governor's document; it was the Indian's treaty, as well – signed by *Tawhee Sockha* Hoontky of the Saponie, *Nehawroose* for the Hoontkymiha of the Stukanocks, *Chaweo* for the Hoontky of the Occoneechee, and *Mawseeuntkey*, Hoontky of the Tottero. They signed a treaty that gave them permission to build for themselves a fort at Christanna. For the Tributary Indians at Christanna, their partnership in constructing the place where all trade south of the James River would pass would bring their people the highly valued trade goods they wanted, and at a fair rate of exchange. And the Fort and their English ally would help protect them from their ancient powerful enemies – the Seneca, the Cayuga, the Genito, and the other Northern Tribes. It is not unreasonable, then, to think that the great Fort at Christanna was a collaborative project, built both by the English and by Indians, each for their own purposes.

The Labor of Trade

Trade at the fort was a driving force for both Spotswood and the Saponie. At Christanna, each pursued trade to advance their separate interests. For Spotswood the centralization of the Indian trade at Christanna would eliminate unfair and provocative English trading practices that resulted in unsettling turmoil and violence. Trade also would bring profits to the stockholders of the Virginia Indian Company and to himself. Profits from the fur trade funded the Fort. Furs were in high demand in

Europe, and the "Act for the Better Regulation of the Indian Trade" of 1713/14 had secured for the Company a 20 year monopoly on the regional fur trade. The Christanna enterprise as a business with investors, however, was predicated upon the use of Indian labor. Fort Christanna was established as a fur trading center, and it was Indian labor almost exclusively that would acquire, transport, and process the hides and furs that brought Christanna its only self-generated income.

Turning Christanna's history around to view the fur trade from the Indian point of view, it is evident that numerous Southeastern tribes saw in Fort Christanna an opportunity to expand their own tribal trade. This was not just Spotswood's frontier enterprise. Indian tribes were eager to participate, and with just as great an entrepreneurial spirit. Christanna was a new and protected source of valuable European trade goods for the Saponie Tribes, the Nottoway, the Meherrin, the Catawba, and others, all eager to acquire new resources and technologies for tribal uses, for their defense, and for their own subsequent trade to other Indian tribes. For the tribes involved, trade at Christanna as set forth in the new treaty would be regular, open to all, and fair. Article VIII read:

> For the conveniency of the said Indians and for the more regular carrying on the trade, there shall be a publick Mart or Fair kept at their Settlement at least six times in a year where it shall be free for all her Majestys subjects to resort with their wares and Merchandizes and to exchange the same with the Indians for their Skins, furrs and other Commoditys, and Magistrates shall be appointed to attend at the Said Fares to see the trade justly managed, to enquire into any abuses or injurys offered to the Indians by any of the English residing among them

and to administer justice in all controversys that may arise between either party concerning the same.

European colonial traders and Governor Spotswood were newcomers to an extensive Indian trading network that predated Columbus by hundreds of years. Fort Christanna, situated as it was near ancient Indian trading paths that ran southwest to the Catawba towns and north into Pennsylvania, was a late development in a broad system of North American Indian trade.[22] As a fur trading center, Christanna brought to many tribes – particularly the southern Virginia Tributary Indians — new occasions to acquire things of value. To understand Christanna fully, it is essential to acknowledge that a centuries-old system of Indian trade made Christanna work as a colonial business venture and made certain tribes willing participants in activities at the Fort.

In his advice to colonial traders in 1670, the explorer John Lederer listed the goods valued highly by trading Indians:

> If you barely designe a Home-trade with neighbour-Indians, for skins of Deer, Beaver, Otter, Wild-Cat, Fox, Racoon, &c. your best Truck is a sort of course Trading Cloth, of which a yard and a half makes a Matchcoat or Mantle fit for their wear; as also Axes, Hoes, Knives, Sizars, and all sorts of edg'd tools. Guns, Powder and Shot, &c. are Commodities they will greedily barter for: but to supply the Indians with Arms and Ammunition, is prohibited in all English Governments.... To the remoter Indians you must carry other kinds of Truck, as small Looking-glasses, Pictures, Beads and Bracelets of glass, Knives, Sizars, and all manner of gaudy toys and knacks for children, which are light and portable. For they are apt to admire such trinkets, and will purchase them at any rate...[23]

By the time Fort Christanna was built, the trade goods desired by Indians had changed. A 1717 law passed by the government of South Carolina listed 30 trade items that Indians had come to prefer. The list is indicative of the kinds of Indian trade goods that passed through Christanna. These included guns, pistols, cutlasses, gunpowder and shot, gun flints, hatchets, tinseled or copper-laced hats, leather girdles (gilt or plain), gartering material, tinseled lace, lacquered or tin buttons, brass beads and wire, copper or brass hawk's bells and horse bells worn in dance regalia, Jew's harps, vermillion and red lead paints used for face and body painting, various types of red and blue cottons, shirting material, red and blue striped Duffield blankets, brass kettles, looking glasses, and scissors. The list of goods the tribes wanted had greatly expanded within one generation.[24] The Indians at Fort Christanna had become deeply engaged in an international trade. It is important to remember that the commodities valued by Indians attained their value within a tribal cultural context. European goods were both physically refashioned and culturally revalued by Indians. Such goods as are found in these lists had many types of worth for Indian people – practical, social, political, and military. It was Indian demand for things of Indian value, however, that generated the trader's commodity list.

John Fontaine was witness to how the tribal part of the bargain worked at Christanna. His entry for April 20, 1716 begins, "About ten in the morning there came to the fort ten of the Meherrin Indians to trade, laden with beaver, deer and bear skins, for our Indian Company [has] goods here for that purpose. They delivered up their arms to the white men of the fort, and left their skins and furs there also."[25] In this instance the burden of labor was literally on the backs of the Meherrin Indians as they transported furs into the Fort. The work that generated all of the resources valuable to Spotswood's Virginia Company – trapping, skinning, scraping, tanning, transporting – was performed by Indians who willingly engaged in the exchange to pursue their own tribal goals. It is the Indian presence at Christanna that created the profit for the Governor's colonial enterprise. Indian labor was Christanna's fundamental resource.

The peltry trade was always at the mercy of the tribes involved. Repercussions from the attack of the Mohawk on the Catawba on April 10, 1717 demonstrates this. After witnessing the rage of the Catawba Indians who suspected English involvement, the Fort's rangers refused to go out beyond its gates out of fear of Catawba reprisal. Traders refused to move their goods, and this brought a halt to trade. Spotswood wrote, "The fear of those still retaining the same Notion that they will revenge themselves on the English, has so possessed the men hyred by the Indian Compa[ny] to guard their cargo that scarce one of them will venture to go out on that service...."[26] He expressed his doubt to the Lords of Trade that any cargo would be traded during the entire summer. As large as the Fort was, and even outfitted as it was with its five 1400-pound cannon and its rangers, the trade at Fort Christanna flowed only when tribes wanted it to flow. Indian trade at the Fort was just that: Indian trade.

There were non-Indian traders, as well, who worked the region southwest of Petersburg all the way to the Catawba villages in what is now South Carolina. John Stewart was one such trader. John Lawson met him at Catawba in 1701 near to where a large Saponie band had built a town on the Yadkin River in Carolina.[27] Lawson's contemporaneous account of Stewart, who in his trade worked with a Saponie assistant, sheds further light on the critical importance of Indian cultural ways, even in trade carried on by non-Indians. Lawson wrote from his English perspective:

> About three in the Afternoon, we reach'd the Kadapau (Catawba) King's House, where we met with one John Stewart, a Scot... who had traded there for many Years... Mr. Stewart had left Virginia ever since the October before, and had lost a day of the Week, of which we inform'd him. He had brought seven Horses along with him, loaded with English Goods for the Indians; and having sold most of his Cargo....
>
> The English Traders are seldom without an Indian Female for his Bed-fellow, alledging these Reasons as sufficient to allow of such Familiarity. First, They being remote from any white People, that it preserves their Friendship with the Heathens, they esteeming a white Man's Child much above one of their getting, the Indian Mistress ever securing her white Friend Provisions whilst he stays amongst them. And lastly, This Correspondence makes them learn the Indian Tongue much the sooner....[28]

For non-Indian traders during this period, intermarriage with Indians delivered keys to success.[29] This frontier practice brought to such traders as John Stewart the good will of the tribes, food and shelter, and critically important trade language skills. From the Indian perspective, all the tribes were aware that strong allies were important in trade as well as in war. Becoming kin was a traditional way to form an alliance. In this regard, the role women played was critical in achieving tribal goals. What was for Lawson a matter of "bed-fellows" and "mistresses" was, for the tribes, a matter of building a lasting relationship that would benefit their people. In contrast to moralistic English attitudes toward sexual behavior, Indian attitudes toward the sexual activities of the unmarried were permissive, and even encouraging, particularly when it was beneficial to tribal interests. The trader's female companion sometimes came with a cost in the form of trade goods given or stolen. Both Lawson and William Byrd II wrote about this cultural practice among tribes of the Piedmont.[30]

In looking at the trade at Christanna, we should be aware that whatever financial gain the Virginia Company achieved at the Fort was built upon the practical mechanisms of trade that were the gatekeepers of English success.[31] The mechanisms of trade at Christanna were defined by tribal customs, tribal values, and tribal success.

The Labor of Defense

Spotswood's need for Indian labor at Christanna did not stop at the construction of the Fort and the ongoing work associated with the peltry trade. It also included the work Saponie Tribes did related to the defense of Virginia. According to the new treaty, the Christanna Tributaries were expected to defend the colonists and the other tributaries from attack by tribes that would threaten them. "The said Indians...shall be ready with all their force to suppress such Conspiracy or foreign Invasion, either by themselves, or in Conjunction with the forces of the said Colony."(Article IV) The use of Tributary Indians as defensive militia enabled Spotswood to save on military expenses. By using his Saponie allies, he was able to disband 9 troops of non-Indian militia and cut the number of colonial militia from 132 to only 24.[32] The work done by Tributary warriors, then, benefitted the Governor's standing with the colonial government, and it defended the colony from those tribes that would threaten it. The Governor's strategy was to defend the colony's frontier as he did at Fort Christanna, with militia accompanied by allied Indians – "Twelve white Men and an Officer, who were designed to be employed to Range, two or three of them at a time, with ten or twelve Indians, and in times of danger frequently to beat the Woods between Settlement and Settlement."[33] The burden on the Tributaries is clear in this ratio.

The Saponie surely recognized that in serving to defend the colony from the incursion of foreign tribes, they would receive provisions, firearms, powder, and shot sufficient for the task. There was no better way to ensure that these European trade goods that were essential for tribal defense and hunting would always remain in good supply. And their defensive task, in league with the English, was to resist the incursion of tribes that were their own longstanding enemies. In becoming a defensive force for Virginia, the Saponie Tribes, in effect, enlisted the English as their ally against the warriors of the Five Nations and the militaristic slaving tribes from the Carolinas. In agreeing to help keep the peace on the colony's southern border, the signatory tribes were not simply acquiescing to English requirements to defend Virginia. The agreement was a strategic move to defend themselves.

In a late chapter in Fort Christanna's history, Governor Spotswood ordered the officer of the Fort, Robert Hix, to engage the Saponie Indians to go into the woods to collect the rangers who had neglected their duties at the Fort, abandoned their posts, and become disobedient. The motivation for the rangers' behavior is not given, but we can imagine that increasing assaults of the Northern Tribes, even on those at the Fort, must have weighed heavily on them. Whatever the reasons for the rangers' disorderly actions, it was the Saponie Tribes that the Governor chose to gather the rangers and return them to their assigned posts. It is clear from this that over time the Saponie warriors came to supersede the rangers as the frontier militia defending the colony.[34]

One Fort, Two Worlds

Primary sources from the period offer few details about Indian and English interaction within the Fort. John Fontaine's 1716 account of his time at the Fort, however, does provides a glimpse of this interaction. He described two events initiated by Governor Spotswood that are particularly noteworthy, as they are evidence of how a new generation of youth at Fort Christanna were beginning to live in two distinctly different cultural worlds.

Perhaps as a display of Indian culture for his guest, John Fontaine, the Governor sent for the young boys of the Indian Town to come to the Fort with their bows and arrows. They arrived and Spotswood organized an archery contest, setting up the eye of an iron axe head as the target. The boys made an impressive display of their skills with the bow, and at a distance of 60 feet from their target, many boys shot arrows through the eye.[35] What lay behind the Governor's diversion is the traditional training the boys had been given in a skill that was useful for hunting and warfare. Though by this time firearms, powder, and shot had replaced the bow and arrow for adult Saponie hunters and warriors, the skills of traditional weaponry were taught to boys. This exhibition of the skill of young archers tells us that fletched arrows, arrowheads, and bows strung with sinew – each with its associated production toolkit – were still a part of the material culture of the Saponie Tribes.

Following the archery exhibition, the Governor asked the boys to perform a "war dance." They called for a singer, and the boys cleared a circle. The singer arrived and took his place in the center of the ring. He sang in an animated way and accompanied himself on a type of drum made of "a piece of board." He beat his drum with "two small sticks," and as he sang, the dancers around him sometimes would call out in response. Not understanding the musical tradition that was behind the indigenous music and dancing he witnessed, Fontaine could only say of it, "Their motions answered in some way to the time of the music." His description of the dancers and their non-European kinds of movement was more elaborate, but predictably Eurocentric and judgmental:

> All that I could remark by their actions was that they were representing how they attacked their enemies, and would relate the one to the other how many of the other Indians they had killed, and how they did it, making all the motions in this dance as if they were actually in the action. By this lively representation of their warring one may see the base way they have of surprising and murdering the one the other and their inhuman way of murdering all their prisoners, and what terrible cries they have when they are conquerers.[36]

For Fontaine, this was a glimpse of the Native style of warfare, as performed by boys. No doubt his extreme critical reaction came, in part, as this type of warfare contrasted sharply with the formalized and restrained European military techniques he had recently experienced as an English foot soldier in Spain – a three-year military adventure in which he saw no action.[37]

The boys who danced for Spotswood, however, knew the ways of the Native warrior. Warfare was a social institution for the tribes of the Southeast. It was the responsibility of Native men and boys to be warriors, to defend their people, and to take revenge on tribal enemies. A young man gained social prestige through his exploits in battle, and through it could earn himself a coveted "warrior's name." [38]

Dancing was associated with warfare, both before and after military conflicts. Dancers enthusiastically mimicked the heroic actions of warriors with gestures and vocal calls. Through dance, males celebrated their social roles and performed their aspirations in ways their communities expected. After a successful military foray, exuberant dancing might continue for days. The celebratory dancing expressed joy of having no casualties, and at the same time, it was an instruction for the young about gender roles, a performance to achieve male status, and a rehearsal for the next battle. Within the Fort the dance was enacted outside of its larger social context, initiated by elders who knew little of its social significance. For Spotswood and Fontaine, the boy's dance was, in the European tradition, an entertainment.

When the dancing and songs were over, the Governor feasted the boys, likely with a meal of pork or beef, and the boys made good work of it. They returned well-fed to the Indian Town, and those archers who had shot arrows through the eye of the axe came home with fine trophies – amazing looking-glasses made in Europe and new knives with metal blades.

CHAPTER FOUR

Place, Lives, and Meanings

Most of those who became the Fort Christanna Indians moved to their new homeland from an earlier settlement known as *Unotee*. It was situated a little more than 30 miles east of what would become the Fort site. The Iroquoian-speaking Meherrin formerly lived at that place and had called it *Unotee*, meaning "hill."[1] On July 29, 1708, following the Saponie tribe's move from mountains in the west, the tribe petitioned the Virginia Council under the terms of the Treaty of Middle Plantation for the unoccupied land at *Unotee*:

> This day the King of the Saponie Indians attended the President and Council and in the name of that Nation presented a petition praying that the said Indians might be received under the protection of this Government they being willing to become Tributarys thereto, Whereupon the Council finding that the said Indians were once Tributarys and included in the Articles of peace agreed at Middle plantation the 29th of May 1677...are of Opinion that it is for her Maj_tys Service that the said Indians be received into the protection of this Government as Tributaries....And whereas the said Indians have

desired that land may be allowed them for their Settlement either in the Forks of three Creeks or the land between Unotee and Reeve's quarter the Council were please to agree to the said desire...[2]

The Saponie and Occoneechee soon settled on the Meherrin at the *Unotee* tract. In 1712 the Tottero petitioned to join the other tribes there.[3]

The provisions of Spotswood's Treaty of 1713/14 put an end to the tribal settlement at *Unotee*. It called for the tribes at *Unotee* to relocate to a new homeland to avoid the conflicts associated with the expanding English colony. In less than a year they had done so. Spotswood reported in a letter to London the following January that the Saponie, Occoneechee, Stukanocks, and Tottero had moved immediately to Christanna after the boundaries of the land were laid out and the rangers were in place.[4] Following their removal only the tribal names remained on the *Unotee* land – "Occoneechee Swamp," "Stewkes Branch" for the Stukanocks, and "Saponi Old Fort." Colonial patents document that from 1717-1723 the land these tribes vacated at *Unotee* was parceled out to colonists in 14 tracts.[5]

The New Town: Chunkete Posse

By the spring of 1716 the Christanna Tributaries had built a new town on their new tract of land. John Fontaine, an observant and curious visitor to Christanna, walked out of the Fort on the fourth day of his stay there and headed downhill to visit the Indians' town that was situated in close proximity to the fort, on a plain by the Meherrin River. His trek took him around the circular form of the town, and he recorded that it had three entrances. The town plan included a stump in the central plaza from which leaders could speak to the people. Fontaine observed that all of the houses were situated inside the protective wall of the place. They were built flush to one another in such a way that their solid back walls together formed the town's palisade – the contiguous houses themselves were the defensive wall. It was clearly a town built by a people with enemies, and though it was different from Fort Christanna, the wall-enclosed Indian town with its houses facing inward shared some similarities with the nearby English structure.[6]

Before his visit to Christanna, John Fontaine had seen traditional Saponie-style houses that were different from these. He had seen rounded houses made of bent saplings and shingled with layers of bark.[7] Fontaine's contemporary, the Virginian Robert Beverley, described that earlier type of house in his book *The History and Present State of Virginia* (1705): "...They stick Saplins into the ground by one end, and bend the other at the top, fastening them together by strings made of fibrous Roots, the rind of Trees, or the green Wood of the white Oak, which will rive into Thongs. [The houses] are covered with the Bark of Trees, which will rive off into great flakes." [8]

At Christanna, however, their architecture had changed. Instead of sticking sharpened saplings into the ground, as was traditional, the tribes at this Saponie town had begun building with sharpened squared timbers. Roofs for the houses were still being made in the traditional way, though, with overlapping layers of peeled oak or hickory bark and a smoke hole in the center. A central fire burned in the houses for warmth and cooking. Beverley's earlier account of the interior of Indian houses is a good description of what Fontaine must have seen. He wrote, "Their Houses or Cabbins, as we call them, are...continually Smoaky, when they have a Fire in them; but to ease that inconvenience, and to make the Smoak less troublesome to their Eyes, they generally burn Pine, or Lightwood, (that is, the fat knots of dead Pine) the Smoak of which does not offend the Eyes, but smuts the Skin exceedingly..." [9]

Fontaine observed beds that were raised like benches two feet off the ground and positioned around the fire. Woven mats divided the interior of the houses. European trade goods had not yet replaced the hand-made pots and wooden dishes he saw. Fontaine reckoned that 200 Indians must have lived in the place, though 300 may have been a better estimate.[10]

Outside the walls of the town, Fontaine took interest in several small structures close to the riverside. They were constructed of hardened clay and were only large enough for one person. Fontaine learned that these structures had an important function in traditional Saponie medicine:

> They call those houses sweating houses, for when they have any sickness they get 10 or 12 pebble-stones which they make very red in a fire and when they are hot they carry them in those little huts and the sick man or woman goes in naked, only a blanket with him and they shut the door upon them and there they sit and sweat until they are no more able to support it and then they go out naked and immediately jump into the water over head and ears. This is the remedy they have for all distempers.[11]

Sweating houses were a common feature at the traditional Siouan villages. They were observed by Hugh Jones at Christanna and earlier by John Lawson at the Siouan town of Sapona.[12] A central sweat house was discovered in the archaeological excavation at the Fredricks site in Hillsborough, NC, the place thought to be the location of the Occoneechee (Achonechy) Town Lawson visited in 1701.[13]

Though the exact location of Christanna Fort is now well known, the location of the Saponie town has eluded historians and archaeologists and has long faded from tribal memory.[14] Several kinds of evidence point to its location, however:

1) First are the details from John Fontaine's *Journal*. In it he describes the "Saponey Indians" as living "within musket shot of this fort," and elsewhere he writes "After breakfast I went down to the Saponey Indian town, which is about a musket shot from the fort. This town lieth in a plain by the river." Since he does not mention that he rode to the town, the town was apparently in walking distance. Fontaine's later account of his departure from the Fort, with the Governor, includes this additional information: "We were just out of the fort when the cannon fired. We passed down by the Indian town...." And the journal entry continues, "After we had rid about a mile we came to a ford of Meherrin River...." They crossed the river with their Saponie guides and continued their return trip to Williamsburg. The Indian town, then, is described by John Fontaine as being a short distance from the Fort, on a plain by the Meherrin River, downhill from and on the same side of the river as the Fort.[15]

It is useful to clarify the period meaning of the term "musket shot," when used as a measure of distance. Though a modern reader may think of it as a general and non-specific description, in the eighteenth-century the term had a fairly specific military meaning. In Lewis Lochée's *Elements of Field Fortification,* published in 1783, the writer defines "musket shot" as 300 yards.[16] In *An Introduction to the Art of Fortification* from 1745, John Brindley wrote: "The Length of a Line of Defence is limited in Fortification, by the ordinary Distance of a Musket Shot, which is about 120 Fathom, (720 feet or 240 yards), and almost all the Military Architecture is regulated by this Rule for the Length of the Defence."[17] Abel Boyer was a contemporary of Spotswood and Fontaine, and a noted chronicler of the reign of Queen Anne. His work from 1701 on fortified towns and the architecture of fortification defined "musket-shot" as 750 feet.[18] Though in the eighteenth-century there was some variation in the distance defined by the term "musket-shot" (240-300 yards), it had a clear military significance with regard to the spacing of assault lines and the construction of defensible fortifications. Important for understanding the location of the Saponie town, Fontaine's use of "within musket shot of this fort" tells us the Saponie Town was only 720-900 feet away from the Governor's Fort.

2) The Native name for the Indian town provides additional clues as to its location. Governor Spotswood called the place "Christ-Anna," but the Saponie had their own name for it. In their Siouan language the name was recorded as "*Chunkete Posse*," literally meaning "Horse Head." John Fontaine recorded in his journal nearly four dozen Saponie words and phrases, together with their English meanings, as he was taught them by the School Master of Christanna, Charles Griffin.[19] In this word list was the phrase, "*Hodke tock ire chunkete posse,*" which he translated as "Is this the way to the horse head." This may

have been a reference to a land feature, to the shape of a bend in the river, or to now-lost cultural information. This Saponie name for the place can be found in Brunswick County, Virginia records until as late as 1792, referring apparently both to the town and to a road that led to the town. The English struggled with the spelling of this indigenous place name, but long after Christanna was abandoned, the Saponie name for the place continued to be spoken even by the Anglo-Americans. In Road Orders it was spelled as *Chunketapusso*.[20] In the Saint Andrews Parish processioning records the town name was recorded 31 times from 1735-1792, spelled variously as Junkatapouse, Jounkatapouse, Junckatapurse, Jackatapurse, Junckataourse, and Juckatapurse.[21] These processioning records refer to roads of the period that connect with each other. Certain of these records point the reader to either the Indian town *Chunkete Posse* or the road that led to it. Combined with basic knowledge of historic Brunswick roads and creeks, the following example from the processioning records is revealing:

> Processioners:
> Edward Robinson, Francis Stainback, and Nathaniel Green from the mouth of the Great Creek to the mouth of the Reedy Creek to the new Courthouse Road near the Widow Edwards to Smoaky Ordinary Road to Junckatapurse Road to the Great Creek. 5 Sep 1755[22]

The three men mentioned in the record had been appointed by the vestry to work with landowners in a specified area in order to verify property lines. The precinct they were responsible for was bounded by land features and roads. Beginning at the mouth of Great Creek, the outline of the land for which they were responsible extended down the Meherrin River to the mouth of Reedy Creek, then continued in a counterclockwise sequence northward to the well-known Smoaky Ordinary Road that intersected with Junkatapurse Road, that turned down and back to cut across Great Creek. The repeated patterns of several successive processioning records indicate clearly that Junkatapurse Road crossed Great Creek and must have continued in a southwest direction toward the location of the Indian town. An 1864 map of Brunswick County depicts what may be a surviving portion of the Junckatapurse Road. [Appendix: V]

3) Historic topographical maps of the area immediately northeast of the fort site also give valuable information about the town's location relative to the fort. One such map shows a road that leads downhill from the fort site, and crosses the Mehrrin River at a location called "Jones Low Bridge."[23] This crossing is approximately a mile from the fort site. Because it is likely that a bridge would have been built where formerly there was a ford in the river, the topographical maps suggest that this is a possible location where Fontaine and the Governor forded the Meherrin with their Saponie companions on horseback. We recall that Fontaine wrote in his Journal: "After we had rid about a mile we came to a ford of Meherrin River...." [Appendix VI]

4) A letter from 1720 offers a final clue related to the town's location. It describes Saponie cornfields "close to the fort." The letter reports that the Indians "sallied out," presumably from the Fort, "and a skirmish ensued." The description does not mention the Saponie town. At that time in the Fort's history the Saponie may have been living within the Fort for defensive reasons. Indians

planted cornfields near to their towns, however, so it is reasonable to conclude that the town must be near the Fort as well.[24]

These strands of information, when taken together, point to the location of the Saponie town, *Chunkete Posse*. Based on the information available, the town was situated downhill and within 1000 feet of the Fort, and in a flat plain near the river. This is consistent with the statement of archaeologist Mary Beaudry, who led excavation work at Fort Christanna from 1979-81. Regarding the location of the Saponie town at Christanna, she concluded, "It is believed to be deeply buried under the alluvial deposits because of its presumed location on the flood plain."[25] Though three centuries of river sediment may have hidden *Chunkete Posse* from subsequent generations, the deep blanket of silt from the Meherrin may also have preserved in sand a pristine record of the town.[26] The Saponie's lost town awaits discovery.

Different Ways: Clothing and Status

Another Saponie phrase in John Fontaine's short vocabulary list was *machneto dusas*, meaning "wig."[27] The English powdered wig, a symbol of status and hierarchy in eighteenth-century Williamsburg, had made its way west to the remote fur trading center, and by 1716 the word "wig" had entered the tribal vocabulary. How alien the English regalia and wearing apparel must have been to the Tributary Tribes at Christanna who did not know the coded social meanings that came with that clothing. The assertion of social rank, power, and intention that was expressed through the wearing of wigs, multi-buttoned coats, waistcoats with wide pocket flaps and matching breeches, cravats, stockings, cutlasses, heavy leather jackboots, and gloves was a new reality for those Tributaries who had not travelled among the English settlements. The Indians at Christanna gave these new things Indian names. In addition to *"machneto dusas,"* Fontaine recorded the Indian words for stockings (*"honis"*), breeches (*"lonoughte"*), coat (*"opockhe"*), shirt (*"opockhe hassa"*), cutlass or sword (*"impough"*), and hat (*"apato bokso"*).[28]

The same was true, of course, for the English who had not interacted with the Indian tribes of the region. Those English had no real understanding of the social and political meanings of Indian regalia and adornment, and their descriptions of Indian clothing reveals this. Hugh Jones, the Anglican minister who visited Christanna, regarded the alien Indian regalia, hair styles, and adornment with dismissiveness and derision:

> Their Hair is very black, course and long; and they are all over daubed frequently with Bear's Oil.
>
> Each Nation has some distinguishing Mark, especially in the Cut or Tie of their Hair, in which they are very whimsical and comical.
>
> They often wear Shells hanging upon their Breasts, with Feathers or a Deer's tail in their bored Ears or hair, with a Wolf or Fox-Skin for a Snapsack; with other odd Accoutrements.
>
> In their Opinion, they are finest when dressed most ridiculously or terribly....
>
> When they are very fine, you may see some of them with their Hair cut off on one Side, and a long Lock on the other. The Crown being crested and bedaubed with red Lead and Oil; their Forehead being painted white, and it may be their Nose black, and a Circle of Blue round one Eye, with the Cheek red, and all the other side of the Face yellow, or in

> some such fantastical manner. These Colors they buy of us, being persuaded to despise their own, which are common and finer.[29]

John Lawson, who visited the Saponie in 1701, wrote that bear's oil was applied beginning at infancy to help the people "better to Endure the extremity of the weather."[30] As for the men's clothing, Jones noted:

> They commonly wear a Dear-Skin, putting their Arms thro' the Holes of the Shoulder, with a Flap ty'd before and behind to cover their Nakedness; though they buy often *Matchcoats* or Blankets now, to defend them from the Wet and Cold, and think themselves very fine in such Coats as our common Soldiers wear, or of any taudry Colours: Besides this, some pin Pieces of red or blue Cloth about their legs, and make *Moccasons* or leather purses for their feet, with which they can travel in the woods, without danger of thorns or stumps.[31]

John Fontaine's journal offers an additional view of the apparel and skin painting of the Christanna Tributaries. In it the writer observed that face and hair painting and regalia of the sort Hugh Jones described was meant to convey a particular social message. Fontaine wrote in his journal a description that was similar to what the cleric had written, but Fontaine noted the display had to do with warfare.

> About three of the clock came fifty of the young men with feathers in their hair, and run through their ears, and their faces painted with blue and vermilion, and their hair cut in many forms, Some left one side of their hair on, and others had their hair cut on both sides and on the upper part of the head, made it stand like a cock's comb, and they had blue and red blankets wrapped about them. They dress themselves after this manner when they go to war the one with the other so they call this their war

dress, which really is very terrible and makes them look like so many furies. Those young men made no speeches, only walked up and down and seemed to be very proud of their abominable dress.[32]

Without resorting to words, warriors spoke clearly through the concrete and powerful language of their regalia.

Hugh Jones noted another feature of Native body marking, observing that tattooing was a common practice. He wrote that "some have their Skins all over curiously wrought with bluish lines and Figures, as if done with Gun-powder and Needles."[33] Referred to by Europeans as "pouncing," "pricking," "marking," or "burning," indigenous tattooing left permanent marks in the skin, and this was often supplemented by skin painting that was temporary. Southeastern Indians tattooed variously with sharpened bone needles, thorns, pointed flint gravers, stone bladelets, slivers of rivercane, or the teeth of fish. The artist drew the tattoo design onto the recipient's face, torso, legs, or arms, according to tribal traditions, then pierced the skin repeatedly along the lines of the design. Tattoo pigment was most often powdered charcoal or ash applied dry or wet onto the punctured skin. Typically an indelible black or bluish line design remained after the skin healed, though sometimes a colored pigment such as ocher or vermillion was used. It is clear from the historical, ethnographic, and archaeological record that tattooing was a widespread practice in Eastern North America, dating back at least as early as the first-century.[34]

What Hugh Jones regarded as curiously wrought lines and figures on skin was important socio-religious information for the tribes interacting at Christanna. For

Indian people, tattoos were permanent and public identifiers for men and women of an individual's tribal and kinship identity. Additionally, design elements might symbolize powerful spiritual beliefs or display the prowess of a warrior. More than simple adornment, from the Native perspective, a tattoo telegraphed information to any approaching viewer regarding an individual's relationship to the spirit world, who his people were, and what his or her rank was within the tribe. Native tattoos were carefully constructed markings of power.[35]

Jones did recognize to some degree that Indian leaders displayed their wealth and status through the wearing of certain kinds of regalia. He observed that, "Every small Town is a petty Kingdom govern'd by an absolute *Monarch*, assisted and advised by his *great Men*, selected out of the gravest, oldest, bravest, and richest; if I may allow their Dear-Skins, *Peak* and *Roenoak* (black and white Shells with Holes, which they wear on Strings about their Arms and Necks) to be Wealth."[36] Jones did not understand the full economic and political significance of those strung shells for Native people. Called *wampum* by other tribes, those strands were a device used by tribal leaders to make binding intertribal trade agreements and alliances. *Wampum* strands and belts were the concrete tools of diplomacy for people who did not negotiate with written words and treaties.[37] Presenting strands or belts of *wampum* in negotiations called for truthfulness and sincerity. Strands were sometimes used as memory devices in public speaking or in reciting the terms of an agreement. Regarded as a spiritual item, *wampum* was thought to be a medicine that could clear the mind of negative things. Displaying it guaranteed safe passage for messengers. Though *wampum* was sometimes used as a valuable trade item, it is not likely that the individuals Hugh Jones observed wore strands of *"Peak* and *Roenoak"* as simply a show of wealth. Wearing such strands was a public display of authority and the capacity to be a dealmaker. The spiritually charged strands of black and white shell represented political power, a more valuable thing for Native leaders than wealth.[38]

Later, William Byrd II recognized, as Jones had, that certain clothing of the Saponie leaders was reserved for important political occasions. He wrote in his *Diary* that, "All the Grandees of the Sappony nation did us the Honour to repair hither to meet us, and our worthy Friend and Fellow Traveller, Bearskin, appear'd among the gravest of them in his Robes of ceremony." [39] Byrd's diary provides no details about what Bear-skin chose to wear to that meeting, and nothing about what Bear-skin wanted to express through his wearing of ceremonial clothing on that day.

We would expect that Headmen from *Chunkete Posse* displayed their status and identity as warriors by wearing enemy scalps. Hugh Jones reported that warriors wore scalps "on a Thong by their side as a signal Trophee and Token of Victory and Bravery."[40] Young men entered into manhood and increased their status by taking scalps they later wore as badges of honor. But for Native people a scalp meant more than simply the proof of a warrior's kill. Many tribes understood that a scalp had a religious significance and represented the ongoing spiritual identity of the victim. More than seizing a war trophy, scalping was an act that captured the spirit of the enemy. Possessing a scalp was understood to deny the dead individual a transition to the afterlife. Scalps had corporate meanings, as well, for towns and kinship groups. Tribes displayed them in public places as signs to the larger community that retributive justice had been served through strength, and balance was restored. Scalps were ritually preserved, mounted and dried on hoops, painted with red pigments, displayed on spears or sticks during the return from a fight, tied to prominent ceremonial poles in villages, and displayed on houses. So the scalps worn by Indians at *Chunkete Posse* conveyed many levels of indigenous meaning, much of which apparently was not comprehended by English observers.[41]

In the first quarter of the eighteenth-century, a newly acquired item was becoming a part of the Saponie's tribal show of status: the horse. Horses were not native to North America at the time of European contact, and they were not part of the traditions of the indigenous peoples in Virginia until they were introduced to the region by Europeans. The word for "horse" in the Saponie language translates literally as "big dog," reflecting the novelty of this new animal to Native people in the Southeast.[42] Fontaine reports that on his return trip home, the Governor allowed the elder in his Saponie escort party to ride the lead horse as a gesture of respect. The man rode the horse with difficulty and was thrown from it once, before eventually returning it to the Governor with complaints about horses.[43] By 1728, however, when "All the Grandees of the Sappony Nation" had occasion to meet William Byrd II, he was impressed that most of the Tributary leaders had come on horseback, even though it was difficult for them to retrieve and ride the horses. According to Byrd it was an act that was "certainly intended for a Piece of State," meaning that it was a political statement of their rank, and it was certainly in imitation of the English.⁴⁴ In 1701 John Lawson's observations confirm that owning and displaying horses was a matter of rank and status. He mentions that horses were owned by Indian "Kings," and he wrote that the "old King" of Sapon (the Saponie town on the Yadkin River) made a point to show Lawson's party his two horses.⁴⁵

John Fontaine described to some degree the attire of women at Christanna, a subject the Rev. Hugh Jones did not mention perhaps out of a sense of clerical modesty. Concerning the Indian women at Christanna the journal writer observed:

> They all have long straight black hair which comes down to their waist. They had each of them a blanket tied about their waists, and it hung down about their waists like a petticoat. They have no shifts or any thing to cover them from their waists up, but go naked. Others of them there was that had two deer skins sewed together and they threw it over their shoulders like a mantle. They all of them grease their bodies and head with bear's oil, which with the smoke of their cabins gives them an ugly hue.⁴⁶

Apparently the aesthetic effect of bear's oil and smoke was no deterrent to Fontaine. Saponie phrases he chose to preserve in his 45-item Indian word list include "How d'ye do," "Will you kiss me," "Come to bed," and "What you please." The word list suggests that the Irish Huguenot visitor may have been aware of the practice of many tribes of offering to traders or prominent visitors a female companion to express hospitality and encourage kinship alliances.⁴⁷

Fontaine and Jones mentioned another visible aspect of women's lives at Christanna – one related both to the care of children and to the work women did. Both reported that the women at Christanna carried their infant children tied to cradleboards. Fontaine observed in his Journal, "The head or top of the board is round, and there is a hole through the top of it, through which there is a string so that when the women are tired holding of them or have a mind to work they hang the board...to a limb in a tree or to a pin in a post for that purpose, and there the children swing about and divert themselves." [48]

Cradleboards must have been a frequent sight at and around the Saponie Town, as women had many gender-specific duties in addition to the care of infants. The cradleboard itself was constructed so the mother could do additional work. Hugh Jones commented on the work he saw women do in contrast to the responsibilities of men: "The Women do all of the hard Labour, such as cutting down the Trees, planting Corn, &, carrying Burthens and all their other work; the Men only hunting, fishing and fowling, eating, drinking, dancing and sleeping."[49]

We have no account from Christanna that describes how women's clothing and adornment may have indicated rank within their society, or what their own "robes of ceremony" might have been. Perhaps future archaeology will reveal something about that, but regarding those aspects of women's lives at Christanna, the primary written sources regrettably are silent.

The Meaning of Red

Early in their interactions with Native peoples, English traders and adventurers recognized that red-colored materials and objects were highly valued throughout the Southeast. Traders benefitted well from the trade of red Stroudwater blankets, various red pigments and paints, and red items of clothing. Fontaine, Jones, Lawson, Beverley, and Byrd make frequent references to red blankets, red pieces of cloth, red lead paint, and vermilion (a scarlet pigment derived from cinnabar) in connection with their descriptions of Native people and trade. Such items regularly brought in a disproportionately high number of hides in the peltry exchange with Indians. A 1718 record from South Carolina of the exchange rate for trade goods and pelts reveals how scarlet-colored things translated into profit for traders.[50] For the Indian traders, a pound of vermilion was worth as much as a gun. A "Pound Vermillion" and "two Pounds red Lead" mixed would fetch 20 pounds of the best deerhides, making those red pigments together the most expensive item on the traders' exchange list. It was worth as much as a gun and two pounds each of shot and powder, and that at a time when all Indian men in the Southeast were hunting and making war primarily with firearms. In addition to vermilion and red lead, other red-colored trade items on the list included woven Stroud blankets and another scarlet woolen called Caddice. [Appendix VII]

For Hugh Jones the high appeal of these commodities had to do with Indian fondness for things "of any taudry Colour."[51] The real reason for the preference for red, though, ran much deeper than the Anglican minister understood. For Southeastern tribes, red was a spiritual color, associated by many tribes variously with the Sun, with fire, with blood, with warfare, and with success. Charles Hudson, in his classic survey, *The Southeastern Indians*, highlights the various tribal uses of red pigment. It was carried in pouches with crystals associated with the Sun, and used ceremonially to ensure good hunting.

Red was the color of the warrior – war clubs were painted red, and red flags were raised and tilted toward enemies. Warriors painted their bodies with red. Priests sprinkled war medicine from red-painted gourds when a new war Chief was being initiated. Dead War Chiefs lay in state with their faces painted vermilion, as red poles with red hoops were raised, symbolizing enemies he had killed. Vermilion was used in tattooing that featured Sun-images, animals, and images depicting military action. Scalp locks were sometimes wiped with red pigment. Red and white were often used in a symbolic opposition to each other. In the great Southeastern spiritual ballgames, whole towns or moieties competed against each other as Red versus White, the White being the team of the Great Sun, the Red being the team of the Great Warrior. Red pigment was an important burial good for those of high rank. Generalizations about Southeastern tribal beliefs can be problematic; symbolic meanings and cultural associations varied among the tribes. It is clear, however, that the symbolism of the color red was part of a broadly held belief system that cut across tribal and even linguistic lines.[52] Of all the colors of body paint used in the Southeast, red is the color most often mentioned.[53]

John Lawson visited the Saponie in 1701 when they lived at the headwaters of the Yadkin River, and he stayed for a while with their Siouan cousins. His *New Voyage to Carolina* includes firsthand accounts that demonstrate the Siouan uses of the red color.

> Amongst the Bears Oil (when they intend to be fine) they mix a certain red Powder, that comes from a Scarlet Root which they get in the hilly Country, near the Foot of the great Ridge of Mountains, and it is no where else to be found. They have this Scarlet

> Root in great Esteem, and sell it for a very great Price, one to another.
>
> With this and Bears Grease they anoint their Heads and Temples, which is esteem'd as ornamental, as sweet Powder to our Hair. Besides, this Root has the Virtue of killing Lice, and suffers none to abide or breed in their Heads. For want of this Root, they sometimes use Pecoon-Root, which is of a Crimson Colour, but it is apt to die the Hair of an ugly Hue.[54]

Lawson elsewhere describes the battle dress of the warriors he saw, and he includes details of their use of red coloring.

> Their Dress in Peace and War, is quite different. Besides, when they go to War, their Hair is comb'd out by the Women, and done over very much with Bears Grease, and red Root; with Feathers, Wings, Rings, Copper, and Peak, or Wampum in their Ears. Moreover, they buy Vermillion of the Indian Traders, wherewith they paint their Faces all over red, and commonly make a Circle of Black about one Eye, and another Circle of White about the other, whilst others bedawb their Faces with Tobacco-Pipe Clay, Lamp-black, black Lead, and divers other Colours, which they make with the several sorts of Minerals and Earths that they get in different Parts of the Country, where they hunt and travel.[55]

During his journey, at the Carolina town of the Waxhaws, Lawson witnessed a striking arrival. "The first day that we came amongst them, arriv'd an Ambassador from the King of Sapona [i.e., King of the Saponie, who were then living on the Yadkin] to treat with these Indians about some important Affairs. He was painted with Vermillion all over his Face, having a very large Cutlass stuck in his Girdle, and a Fusee [pistol] in his Hand."[56]

So the widespread symbolic use of the color red was a part of the Siouan tradition of the Christanna Tributaries, as well. It was important enough to the Virginia Tributary Tribes that Article VII of the Treaty of Middle Plantation included provisions allowing for gathering *"Puckoone"* (Lawson's "Pecoon-Root," *Sanguinaria canadensis*). It is unfortunate that there was no observer at Fort Christanna who inquired about the cultural meaning of the color for the Saponie Tribes. The accounts of Jones and Fontaine, whose observations were colored by their European expectations and priorities, did not include any discussion with the Tributaries regarding the importance of the prominent color. The two Englishmen were culturally colorblind to the larger symbolic significance of the red they saw.

One piece of Saponie testimony does exist, however, regarding the cultural importance of the red pigment. In 1728, years after the Fort had been abandoned by the English, William Byrd II passed near Christanna on his trek to establish for the first time an official dividing line between the colonies of Virginia and North Carolina. Realizing that those who traveled with him were not sufficiently competent at hunting for their food, Byrd sent the translator Charles Kimball to Christanna, where the Saponie were still living. His instructions were to bring back men who would be hunters for the party. In the end only one Saponie man would be their hunter and guide. Byrd did not record the man's name in the Saponie language, but he referred to him by his hunting-name – "Bear-skin."[57]

Byrd wrote in his account that on the third day after Bear-skin joined the survey party, they came to a large creek "which the Indians call'd *Massamoni*, signifying, in their language, Paint-Creek, because of the great Quantity of Red ochre found in its banks." [58] We can be sure that it was Byrd's Saponie guide who provided the surveyors with the name *"Massamoni"* and its explanation. Linguistic evidence also tells us that *Massamoni* was a Saponie language place name. A vocabulary list from Fort Christanna includes the Saponie word *"money,"* meaning "water." Byrd wrote down several other creek names in Saponie territory, and these have in common the same Saponie root word for water – *Ohimpa-moni* or Fishing Creek, *Hicootomoni* or Turkey-Buzzard River, and *Tewaw-homminy* or Dead Tuscarora Creek.[59] In this clearly Siouan name, *Massamoni*, the Saponie people had stated, "We use this red earth as paint."

The fifty young Saponie men, then, who came to Fort Christanna following the attack by the Genito, came in the warrior tradition, their faces painted with red and ash. They came and stood silently in their Stroud trade blankets of red and blue, in a display of their prowess. Their people had been given powder and shot by the Governor, so the young men, the warriors, came to present themselves to their benefactor as a force of worthy and brave allies. Their faces and hair were oiled and painted with vermilion or with the red earth from *Massamoni*, Paint Creek. They were in their finest battle dress, protected and empowered by a sacred color.

CHAPTER FIVE

The Idea of the Indian School

Governor Spotswood's 1713/14 Treaty with the Saponie Tributary Tribes included a key provision for religious education of Indian children. Spotswood was not the first in Virginia to be concerned with the education of Indians, however. As early as 1618 the Virginia Company of London directed Governor Elect George Yeardley to build a college at Henrico "for the training up of the Children of those Infidels in true Religion moral virtue and Civility and for other godly uses."[1] Anglican Church Vestry in many Virginia parishes frequently required that Indian indentures and orphans be given both religious education and instruction in reading.[2] Legislation that was enacted during the period before Spotswood required that education be a part of the care given to Indian hostages. A portion of a 1663 Act related to Indian matters reads: "It is alsoe enacted that the hostages to be delivered shal[l] be civilly used and treated by the English whose charge they shall be delivered, and that they be brought up in the English literature."[3]

The powerful and persuasive Rev. James Blair, the Anglican Bishop's representative in America, fought successfully for Indian education through the establishment of the College of William and Mary. A phrase from the beginning of the 1693 Charter for the College articulated an aspect of its mission – "That the faith may be propagated amongst the Western Indians, to the glory of Almighty God." This initiative gained momentum during the time Christanna was an active English project. The legacy from the estate of English scientist Sir Robert Boyle, who was Blair's uncle, made Indian Schools possible at Harvard College and at The College of William and Mary. The Boyle funds that came to Virginia were sufficient initially to provide room and board and instruction for up to 10 Indian students. The Indian students there were given instruction in religion, reading, writing, and "all other arts & sciences, that the best Englishmen's sons do learn." It was Blair's hope that educated Indians could, in turn, be sent out to convert other Indians.[4]

In 1699 James Blair penned a "Proposition for the Christian Education of Indians, Negroes, and Mulatto Children." Though the Proposition was not published until 1727, it reveals much about the spirit of the time and the thought of Virginia's religious and political leaders. Blair's interest in the education of Indians was primarily a concern for religious instruction and conversion. The Proposition begins:

> It being the duty of Christianity, very much neglected by masters and mistresses of this country to endeavor the good instruction and Education of their Heathen Slaves, in the Christian faith... It is therefore humbly proposed that every Indian, negro, or mulatto child that shall be baptized and

> afterwards brought to church and publicly catechized by the minister and in church before the 14th year of his or her age, shall give a distinct account of the Creed, Lord's Prayer and Ten Commandmts and whose master or mistress shall receive a Certificate from the minister that he or she hath so done, such Indian, negro or mulatto child shall be exempted from paying all levies til the age of 18 years...[5]

The Proposition has an unspoken subtext. In Blair's time, Southeastern Indians were a major portion of the Southern slave population. Alan Gallay has estimated that 30,000-50,000 American Indian men, women, and children were bought or sold in the British slave trade before 1715.[6] James Blair's Proposition reflects the attitudes of a colonial culture that had fully embraced the enslavement of Indian people. What lay beneath the acceptance of owning Indians as property was an economic system that encouraged intertribal warfare for the purpose of capturing prisoners who first were sold by Indians for European trade goods, then resold as slaves.

Another prominent advocate of Indian education was the Royal Governor of Virginia (1698–1705), Francis Nicholson. He was enthusiastic about the idea of Indian education funded by the Boyle legacy. In 1700 he directed traders John Evans and Robert Hicks (Hix), who later would be captain of the rangers at Fort Christanna, to go to the Indian towns and encourage tribal participation in the College. Nicholson gave the traders clear instructions that indicate the level of thought he had put into the plan:

> You shall acquaint them that this next Summer the rooms will be made ready at the College for their reception & accommodation & that if any one Great nation will send 3 or 4 of their children thither, they

> shall have good, valuable clothes, books & learning & shall be well look'd after both in health & sickness & when they are good scholars, shall be sent back to teach the same things to their own people. Let the children be young, about 7 or 8 years of age, seeing they are to be taught from the first beginning of letters....[7]

Governor Nicholson, co-founder with James Blair of the College of William and Mary, was an ardent supporter of numerous religious and missionary efforts in Virginia.[8] A zeal to replace Indian beliefs with Christianity lay behind his efforts to educate Indian children at the College, though he did not want English to replace their Native language. He called for tribal elders to accompany the students and keep them fluent in their Native tongue so the children could eventually return to their towns and carry out their missionary roles.

One early strategy for bringing Indians students to the College was to purchase enslaved children that had been captured in warfare and enroll them in the Indian School there.[9] Another approach to encourage attendance was to release the tribes that sent a required number of children to the College from their obligation to pay their annual tribute in hides to the Governor. In 1711 the new Governor, Alexander Spotswood, seemed jubilant at his success with the enrollment at the Indian School:

> ...the King of the Nansemonds has already sent his son and cousin. The Nottoway and Maherines have sent each two of their chief men's sons to be brought up to learning and Christianity, and the Queen of Pamunky upon seeing how well those Indian children are treated has engaged to send her son and the son of one of the chief men upon the same foot and I also expect another boy from the Chicohominys....the remitting their tribute is one of

The Idea of the Indian School 71

> the conditions for their keeping their children at the College, and I believe a strong motive to engage their compliance....[10]

Certainly the strongest motivation for the tribes was not a change in the tribute, but the reliable access to English trade goods that came with compliance.

By 1712 enrollment at the Indian School at the College of William and Mary had risen to more than twenty students.[11] There was another side to the seeming altruism of the Indian School, however. Drawing on the Indian policies of Virginia Governors as far back as 1656, Spotswood's plan at the College was not only to re-educate the Indian students, but to use the Indian students as hostages.[12] Spotswood's contemporary, William Byrd II, described in hindsight Spotswood's efforts at the College:

> That Gentleman was lieut Governor of Virginia when Carolina was engaged in a Bloody War with the Indians. At that critical Time it was thought expedient to keep a Watchful Eye upon our Tributary Savages, who we knew had nothing to keep them to their Duty but their Fears.
>
> Then it was that he demanded of each Nation, a Competent Number of their Great Men's children to be sent to the College where they served as so many Hostages for the good Behavior of the Rest, and at the same time were themselves principled in the Christian Religion.[13]

The hostage Indian children whose lives were so dramatically changed in this protracted game among Nations, for security, survival, and salvation, are almost forgotten. Only a few of their names are in the surviving records.[14]

Alexander Spotswood embraced the intellectual and spiritual concerns of his predecessors to Christianize and to educate the Indians, and he incorporated their ideas into his larger Indian policy. His evolving ideas about the usefulness of Indian education were codified in the Treaties of 1713/14 and the "Act for the Better Regulation of the Indian Trade." Together, these called for the construction of Indian Schools where the Indians lived, and detailed the requirements placed on the tribes.[15]

In the Treaty with the Saponie Tributaries, Article II addressed Indian education at Christanna, and Article V earmarked an amount of land within the 36 square mile tract for the use of a School Master, a Minister, and the militia at the Fort.

> The said Indians do consent and promise that as soon as a Tract of Land shall be alotted them for their habitation, and a School Master and Minister established among them, all their Children, and also the Children of any other Nation of Indians who shall incorporate with them shall be taught the English language and instructed in the principles of the Christian Religion.
>
> It is hereby concluded and agreed that there may be set apart by the Governour of Virginia out of the land assigned from time to time for the habitation of the said Indians, a tract not exceeding two thousand acres for the better support of the Minister and School Master to be established there, and of the officer and men to be appointed for the Guard of the said Indian fort, which tract shall in like manner remain for the use of the said Minister, School Master, officer and men, according to the distribution thereof to be made for each respectively by the Governour of Virginia.

Continuing the successful approach he took at the College, in Article IX the Governor reduced the tribute gift required of the tribes. Wanting to "encourage and promote the Conversion of the said Indians," Spotswood made compliance with the *Treaty* more attractive by reducing the annual gift of allegiance from 20 hides (a legacy of the Treaty of 1646) to only three arrows.

Spotswood's plan for an Indian School at Christanna aspired to more than conversion and religious education, however. Just as he did at the College, the Governor intended to use the Christanna school and the children there as his tools to pacify the colony's southern frontier. His plan was to require all of the tribes friendly to the English to send children of their best families to be kept at Christanna, in his words, as "hostages." Spotswood's thought was that by holding those children under English control at the Christanna school, he could ensure compliance and peaceable behavior from the Tributary Tribes. Those nations would be the colony's eyes and ears along the southern border of the colony at a time when tribal warfare in the Carolinas had potential to spread. They would be a capable military force for a Governor who had recently found it difficult to raise a wartime militia.

Spotswood saw clearly that the key to tribal cooperation was trade. "The principal Inducement, both to our Tributary Indians and to the Cattabaws (Catawbas), for delivering their Children to be bred Christians, is the promise of goods at cheaper rates."[16] This he provided them. In February 1715/16 Spotswood wrote a letter to the Lords of Trade that reveals how, at Christanna, trade, defense, education, and religious conversion were intertwined:

> The most considerable Nation of 'em are settled on our Frontiers at a fort I have lately built, and w'ch is to be maintain'd by the Gentlemen of the Indian Company...All the Indian trade of this Colony is carryed on at their fort, and the Company have, out of regard to their Permitting their children to be educated in the Christian religion, agreed to furnish them with goods at a Cheaper rate than any other forreign Indians. So that they are well pleas'd with their Circumstances...I doubt not they will both prove a good Barrier on that Quarter against the Incursions of any forreign Indians, and also keep in awe our other Tributarys...if they should at any time be inclinable to give us disturbance, especially when once the Nation is brought over to ye Christian faith which purpose I have, at my own Expence, settled a School Master among them, who has at this time 100 of their Children under his care.[17]

Beneficial terms of trade was not the sole inducement Spotswood and the Council used, however. Their methods also included punitive measures and even kidnapping. When the Nottoway refused to send their twelve children as hostages to Christanna, as required by their 1713/14 Treaty, the Governor had the "Nottoway King" and six Headmen put in shackles for three days to encourage their reconsideration.[18] In response to the disobedience of the Meherrin leaders and their failure to comply with the *Treaty*, the Virginia Council called on the Governor to seize their wives & Children, to be taken to Christanna and "put under the care of the guard there untill such time as the said Indians shall Voluntarily remove themselves to the land which shall be assigned them there."[19] Documents do not tell whether or not this action was taken.

The Nottoway, Meherrin, and the Tuscarora were resistant to the demand for hostages. They apparently

The Idea of the Indian School

never sent their children to the Indian School at Christanna, as their treaties had required. These tribes spoke Iroquoian languages, and the Saponie Tributaries spoke Siouan dialects. There was historic enmity between tribes of different language groups. Iroquoian-speaking tribes shared certain common lifeways, beliefs, and alliances that differed from those of the Saponie. Those differences contributed to age-old conflict and suspicion that often played out with loss of life. The intertribal conflicts and violence recorded at Christanna developed along linguistic lines: the attacks of the Iroquoian-speaking Genito and Five Nations tribes were on the Siouan-speaking Catawba and Saponie. Reciprocal Siouan attacks on Iroquoians followed. Fontaine recorded in his *Journal* that when the Iroquoian-speaking Meherrin brought their load of hides to Fort Christanna to trade, they refused to go into the fort.[20] Presumably this was because of unfriendly relations with the Siouan-speaking tribes that were closely tied to the Fort. Tribal participation at the Christanna school was defined by many factors, but among the most important of these was the cultural rift between tribes who spoke different tongues. The tribal make-up of students at the Indian School was in part defined by the Indian languages they spoke.

CHAPTER SIX

"A Very Handsome School"

The English and the Siouan Tributaries came together on a tract of land "six miles square," but culturally, spiritually, and socially they were worlds apart. The idea of a perfect square of measured land was in its essence dissonant with the land the Tributaries knew – the real terrain of forked creeks, steep banks, ridges and guts, ancient paths, and its central, wandering green river. But there at Christanna and *Chunkete Posse* the Nations came together. There a school was built – a single building, but in a very real way it was two schools, as different from each other as the surveyed square was from the weather-worn earth. It was one school for the English who planned it and taught there, and it was a very different school for the Indian students and the Tribal families who brought their children to it. The stories of both Schools should be told.

The Governor's School

Spotswood had a school built at Christanna at the expense of his Virginia Indian Company. Several tribes eventually would send their children there, but its first pupils were from the Saponie Tributary Tribes, and they always were the largest group of students at the school. This would be expected, since the Saponie had moved their main town to the Christanna land. A more interesting reason has to do with the physical location of the school on the 36 square mile tract of land set aside for the Saponie. A careful reading of the documents that are related to the Christanna school leads to the conclusion that the Indian School was built at the Saponie Town, *Chunkete Posse*, and not at the Fort as some have thought.

There has been a lack of clarity about where the Indian School was located. Part of the confusion about the physical location of the Indian School comes from Spotswood, himself, who sometimes used the term "Christanna" (or "Christ-Anna") in reference to the pentagonal fort, and at other times for the entire 36 square mile area. Consequently, his use of a phrase such as "the School at Christanna" is not a clear locational reference. Charles Griffin, the School-Master at Christanna, is of little help. He wrote from Christanna on January 12, 1716/17 that the Indians received him with kindness, respect, and appreciation for the good the Governor had done "in Sending me to live among them to teach their children."[1] His language could lend itself to either interpretation. And William Byrd II was equally ambiguous when he wrote that Spotswood "Plac'd a School-Master among the Saponi Indians."[2] Neither Griffin nor Byrd tells us where the School was.

Spotswood's initial idea for all the new Indian Schools called for in the Treaties of 1713/14 was to place them in the Indian Towns. He wrote the Bishop of London on July 26th, 1712 in search of support for his future project. "I would humbly offer to Your Lordship to move the Society for propagating the Gospel for one or two Missionarys to reside at the principal towns of the Indians and have a Church or Chappell built there, and a School-house."[3] By 1715 the Christanna Fort and schoolhouse were built, and Spotswood wrote again to the Bishop of London on October 26, "The late erected Indian Company have built a fine School house at one of the Indian towns, and I have settled a Master there."[4] And later in the year Spotswood wrote Governor Hunter of New York of the Saponie: "There are now 100 of them at a school, I have lately set up at their Town."[5] Taken together, the source documents that mention the Christanna Indian School indicate that it was situated within the Indian town, where the School-Master was settled among them.

In addition to documentary evidence, archaeological evidence from the Fort strongly points to the conclusion that the Indian School at Christanna was not in the Fort. If the school with an ongoing presence of 70-100 or more Indian children had been built inside the Fort, the excavation done at the Fort site in 1979-81 and 2001-2004 should have discovered evidence of it. That evidence was not found, however. In fact, very few items clearly associated with historic-period Indians have been discovered inside the outline of the walls at the fort site. These include several pieces of Colono-Indian ware, a few copper tinklers, thumbscrapers used in hide preparation, and one period projectile point. One slate pencil was also found, but more Indian- and school-related artifacts would be expected if the Indian School were in the Fort. The analysis of faunal remains associated with food preparation and refuse at the Fort also argues against a substantial Indian presence in the Fort. If an Indian School had been present, we would expect to find evidence of a corresponding level of consumption of traditional Native foods within the Fort. Analysis of 4032 bone fragments acquired in the first three seasons of excavation at the Fort yielded 238 identifiable domestic animal bone fragments and only 23 fragments identifiable as wild fauna, however. The bulk of the meat consumed by those in the Fort came from pigs, cattle, and goats or sheep, and consumption of these farm animals is typical of the Anglo-European diet.[6] Since the traditional meat of Native peoples came from wild animals, the taxonomic evidence of bone fragments argues to some degree against the presence of the number of Native people that we would expect to be associated with an Indian School in the Fort. The documentary and archaeological evidence we have, then, tells us the school at Christanna was not in the Fort, but in the Indians' town, *Chunkete Posse*.

Charles Griffin, the School-Master at Christanna, was born in England and was probably educated there, but he came to the American Southeast as an immigrant from the West Indies. Before coming to Virginia, he was a schoolmaster in Pasquotank Precinct (Albemarle) in North Carolina. His school was the first recorded school in North Carolina. He was praised both as a lay reader in the Anglican Church and as a teacher.[7] His reputation among churchmen declined, though, following accusations of fornication and "falling into Quakerism."[8]

Griffin left Carolina and settled in Virginia where he made a positive impression. In 1715 Governor Spotswood employed him to teach the Indian children at the Christanna school. William Byrd II later described the Christanna School-Master with considerable appreciation. "The Person that undertook that Charitable work was Mr. Charles Griffin, a Man of good Family, who by the Innocence of his Life, and the Sweetness of his Temper, was perfectly qualify'd for that pious undertaking. Besides he had so much the Secret of mixing Pleasure with instruction, that he had not a Scholar, who did not love him affectionately."[9] Even the Anglican minister Rev. Hugh Jones gave unqualified praise to the Master of the Christanna School: "I have seen Seventy Seven *Indian Children* at a Time at School, under the careful Management of the worthy Mr. *Charles Griffin,* who lived there some Years for that Purpose...The *Indians* so loved and adored him, that I have seen them hug him and lift him up in their Arms, and fain would have chosen him for a *King* of the *Sapony Nation.*"[10]

Griffin was both a teacher and a scholar. On a wet and windy day at Christanna, John Fontaine and Lt. Governor Spotswood entertained themselves indoors by reading the School-Master's manuscript, his "observations on the benefits of a solitary life."[11] Fontaine entered into his *Journal* a valuable list of Saponie words, numbers, and phrases that must have come from the study Griffin had done with the Siouan Tributaries. Griffin came to teach the Indians his words, and they taught him theirs. The School-Master's vocabulary list is a primary source for what is known about the language the Tributaries spoke at Christanna.[12] Hugh Jones, author of *The Present State of Virginia* (1724), gave credit to Griffin for teaching him

"A Very Handsome School"

all he knew about Indians. In time, after funding for Fort Christanna was disallowed, Charles Griffin returned to the College of William and Mary to teach the Indian students there. He was Head-Master of the Indian School in Williamsburg from 1718 -1720. After 1720, Griffin who was not quite 40, disappears from the historical record.

A tantalizing document survives that clearly puts distance between the Indian School and the Fort in later years. In 1721, well after funding for the Fort had been terminated, a land patent for two thousand acres was given to Nathaniel Harrison and John Allen "at the place known by the name of Griffins School, on a Creek about six miles above Fort Christanna in Brunswick County."[13] By the time this 1721 patent was written, Griffin was no longer the School-Master at the Indian School at the College of William and Mary. Though it is not likely we will ever know what happened to the Christanna School-Master in the end, the 1721 patent record suggests the possibility that he returned to the west to teach the Tributaries beyond the far end of the six mile square Saponie Tract.

In Charles Griffin's own description of the Christanna Indian School, Griffin the devout Anglican told what the hostages were being taught:

> We have here a very handsome school built at the Charge of the Indian Company in which are at present taught 70 Indian Children, & many others will be brought hither in the spring to be put under my care in order to be instructed in the religion of the holy Jesus. The greatest number of my scholars can say the belief, the Lord's prayer, and Ten Commds perfectly well, they know that there is but one God & they are able to tell me how many

persons there are in the Godhead & what each of those blessed persons have done for them. They know how many sacraments Christ hath ordained in his Church & for what end he instituted them, they behave themselves reverently at our daily prayers & can make their responses, which was no little pleasure to their great & good benefactor the Govr..."[14]

Alexander Spotswood, the "great & good benefactor" of the student-hostages, conceived the school, had it funded through the Indian Company, oversaw its construction, and paid the School-Master's salary out of his own pocket – £50 per year.[15] To give a sense of the relative value of Griffin's salary, in 1719 Spotswood's annual salary was £2000 per year. Gentlemen of the Virginia Council received £350 and the Clerk of the Council received £100 per annum.[16]

The Indians' School

Spotswood reported June 4, 1715 to the Lords Commissioners of Trade that he had chosen 70 Saponie boys and girls who were an ideal age for learning. Based on the guidelines for the selection of students that Francis Nicholson had specified earlier, one can assume the youngest hostages were 7 or 8 years of age. Knowing only those details, it is worth considering the strangeness of the school environment for those Indian students.

In contrast with the schooling at Christanna, traditional education for the Tributary Indians was gender-specific, as it was for all the Indians of the Southeast. Men were the teachers for boys, and women for girls. Traditional learning was connected with specific roles and jobs defined by gender. Though it is difficult from a modern perspective to imagine tribal roles and tribal work responsibilities being so thoroughly tied to gender, it is important to do that in order to comprehend the Indian children's experience at the Christanna School. As Charles Hudson put it, "The fundamental division of labor among the Southeastern Indians was between men and women," and that was how the traditional culture of the Tributaries was organized.[17] So the educational environment at Christanna, where males and females were taught together and where girls were instructed by a man, was a challenge to tribal roles and traditions.

Women's traditional roles required learning women's skills. Those skills included weaving baskets and mats, making pottery, cooking, keeping a productive garden from spring through fall, girdling trees to clear fields for planting, cooking, gathering wild plants for food and medicine, finishing the treatment of hides, making clothing, in addition to caring for young children. Men, for their part, were concerned with hunting and fishing, tracking, building dugout canoes, carrying on trade, fashioning weapons and tools, mastering the skills of the warrior and the politician, and participating in ceremonial events. Girls and boys learned their respective skills through experience with elders of their same gender.

Being removed from their traditional learning environments, however, and at an age when they normally would learn life skills essential for the tribe, the students at the Christanna School were cut out of the flow of traditional tribal knowledge. Understood in the tribal context, the schooling with Charles Griffin was a disruption in the continuity of their culture. At the Indian School, time formerly spent learning the ways of food gathering and hunting, tool making and cane weaving, was replaced by time spent learning prayers in a foreign language to an unknown God.

The English effort to convert the Christanna students to Christianity was an educational effort to eradicate the traditional spiritual beliefs of the Tributary Tribes. Spotswood dismissed indigenous religious thought as "Savage principles and Heathenish Superstitions."[18] What do we know about the religion of the Saponie Tribes? What Native beliefs did Spotswood's Indian School challenge? Rev. Hugh Jones wrote of the Indians' belief in a god *Mohomny* who lived beyond the Sun.[19] According to Jones, the Indians believed that at death an individual goes to Mohomny and is judged for his behavior during life. If a person lived a good life, his reward was continued life in a land of plenty. If the individual had lived a morally bad life, however, he would be sent to a barren land where hunting was difficult and the prey was poor.[20] Despite being an Anglican clergyman, Jones' knowledge of the Indians' religion was scant, and he wrote very little about it.

Another source that describes traditional Saponie religion is embedded in William Byrd's account of the creation of the Virginia-North Carolina dividing line. Byrd's hunter and guide on that expedition was Bear-skin (or "Ned Bearskin"), a Saponie man who was living at Christanna in 1728. While on the journey with Byrd's survey party, Bear-skin had a lengthy and frank exchange with the Englishman regarding his religion. At that time, openness concerning religious matters was rare for Indians generally. John Lawson had observed in 1701 that the meaning of many ceremonies "they reserve as a

Secret amongst themselves."[21] This was not the case with Bear-skin, however.

Byrd's account of his fireside conversation with Bear-skin is colorful, lengthy, and fraught with hyperbole. It offers more detail than Jones' account of Indian spiritual beliefs, but the two descriptions of Saponie religious ideas are similar in many ways. Byrd reported that the Saponie guide told of his belief in a supreme God and several lower deities. The Master-God created the World and the Sun, Moon, and Stars. According to Bear-skin, this Master-God had destroyed many inferior worlds before creating this one. This God was just, and he protected and rewarded good people in this life. "But all such as tell Lies, and cheat those they have Dealings with, he never fails to punish with Sickness, Poverty, and Hunger, and, after all that, Suffers them to be knockt on the Head and scalpt by those that fight against them."[22]

Bear-skin believed all souls at death travel together for a while until they reach a fork in the road, where the good people are separated from the bad. In Byrd's account, Bear-skin describes a Venerable Elder who evaluates all who pass by, and the idyllic land the good people enjoy. For those who were judged bad, their fate was understood as life in a harsh and tormenting place.

Taken together, the accounts of Saponie religion recorded by Jones and Byrd share a common understanding that in the afterlife there is a judgment by a divine arbiter who sends the good and the bad individuals in separate directions. It is possible that Saponie religious thought had been influenced by Anglican notions of divine judgment of the soul at death. It also may be the case that the two English writers separately infused non-Native, Christianized interpretations into their accounts. But the similarities in the two accounts make it more likely that they were reporting, with some degree of accuracy, that the Saponie did believe in a judgment of the individual by a supernatural being after death. It is worth noting that similar religious ideas of an afterlife involving the journey of the spirit of the dead (ghost path or Milky Way) and the judgment of the dead by a divine being are present in Western Siouan traditions, as well.[23] This suggests that Saponie ideas of the afterlife were ancient Siouan beliefs.

Elsewhere in his account Byrd preserved additional details about traditional Saponie religious and philosophical beliefs that survived the re-education program at the Indian school. In his account of the dividing line journey, Byrd describes Bear-skin's deep concern regarding a particular English food preparation and its religious meaning.

> Our men kill'd a very fat Buck and Several Turkeys. These two kinds of Meat boil'd together...made excellent Soupe.... Our Indian was very Superstitious in this Matter, and he told us, with a face full of concern, that if we continued to boil Venison and Turkey together, we Shou'd for the future kill nothing, because the Spirit that presided over the Woods would drive all the Game out of our sight.[24]

The account of this exchange opens up two important aspects of Bear-skin's Saponie belief system. The first has to do with his complex understanding of the need to keep the opposing forces of the world separate. In the Southeastern Indian worldview, all the things of this world belong to specific categories; things in one

"A Very Handsome School" 87

category exist in contrast and in balance with things in other categories. For example, "Male things" and "Female things" were regarded as being in different categories. "Animals that flew" were in a different category from "animals with four Legs." So it was with water and fire, things of the night and things of the day, and so on.[25]

Understanding the cosmos in that way, Bear-skin considered it right and wise to keep unlike things separated from each other. Doing otherwise resulted in pollution, and it was dangerous. Mixing unlike things – elements, animals, foods, or ceremonies from opposing categories – upset the fundamental balance of things in Bear-skin's Saponie worldview. For Bear-skin, when meats of the four-legged (deer) and winged animals (turkey) were cooked together, a fundamental violation of the principle of separation had been committed. Byrd's Saponie guide knew that dire consequences would result from this polluting act. It would have a negative effect on the success of hunters, jeopardizing the entire journey. Byrd was right to note the Saponie hunter's "face full of concern."

For Bear-skin, the English violation of a fundamental cosmological principle was not just an abstraction. He told Byrd that their act would incur the wrath of the Spirit of the Woods. For the Saponie, no hunter could be successful without the proper prayer and offering to the Spirit Being that allowed success in the hunt. Hunting was, for Bear-skin, a religious act that required proper ceremony as well as skill. Without the encouraged benevolence of the Spirit of the Woods, the best hunter would fail. For Bear-skin and the Saponie, the world was filled with many spirits who must be honored. In contrast with the Native cosmology of Bear-skin's people, Charles

Griffin would teach students that the success of the hunter was a blessing from the One Almighty God. At the Indian School, Saponie traditional beliefs, rituals, and cosmology were under a cultural attack led by the Governor and his School-Master.

In addition to the Saponie tributaries, other tribes were willing to comply with Governor Spotswood's plan for the Indian School. The tribes that showed the greatest willingness to send their children to the Christanna School were Siouan-speaking people. The Catawba and their allies were such a people. These groups shared a certain level of cultural affinity and history with the Saponie. The Saponie had lived near the confederated Catawba villages in 1701 when Lawson visited them, and the people of those towns were certainly already connected with Christanna through the fur trade. According to Robert Beverley (1705) many of these regional tribes used the Occoneechee language as a *lingua Franca* for trade, so the link was linguistic as well as economic.[26] With few cultural obstructions between themselves and the Saponie Tribes, and with an urgent need to find reliable new trading partners in the wake of the wars in the Carolinas, a Catawba alliance at Christanna was desirable – even essential. It was the prospect and the necessity of trade with the English that was their enticement.

That reality lay behind the decision of the Catawba leaders to journey to the Fort in 1717 with Headmen from the "Sutarees, Sugas, Pedees, Quiawaes, Chacees, Saxapahaes, Enoes, and Sawraes."[27] Even after being ambushed by Northern Tribes in the shadow of the Fort, and with a lingering suspicion of the English, the leaders of the Catawba villages were willing to leave their children at Christanna. The minutes of the Council reported that "divers Presents of Powder were made by the Gov[ernor] to the Western Indians at the delivering their Hostages according to the Custom of Treating with those Indians."[28] Their dependence on English trade goods had left them desperate. The men in each Catawba town needed European fire arms, powder, and lead shot for hunting, making war, and defending themselves. Bright blankets had replaced hides for clothing and status. Their preferred tools were now metal, not stone. Without trade the Catawba towns would perish. So the leaders left eleven children at the Christanna School, where for a time they were taught the new religion, and they learned to speak the new trade language – English.

Student presence at the Christanna School expanded over time and must have become a considerable burden on the Saponie Indian Town. In June 1715 Spotswood reported that 70 boys and girls were enrolled at the school. By February 1715/16 the numbers has risen to 100 students. And in April the following year the Catawba Headmen delivered 11 additional children, bringing the total to as many as 111 students. Questions arise relating to how these children were accommodated at Christanna. The Governor's letter in 1715 indicates that the initial 70 boys and girls were from the Saponie Tribes at *Chunkete Posse*. With an understanding that the school was situated in the Indian Town, the simple assumption is that those children were housed and fed in their own family houses. That still leaves 41 children who likely were from other towns. Where did those hostage students stay? There is no archaeological or documentary evidence that any of the children were kept at the Fort. When the Governor wanted boys for an archery exhibition, he called for them to come to the Fort from *Chunkete Posse*. The boys themselves had to send for a singer when a war dance was requested. It is extremely unlikely that men like the twelve rangers of the Fort were the caretakers and cooks for Indian children. Neither is it likely that Charles Griffin, author of "observations on the benefits of a solitary life," could have both taught and tended to the needs of up to 41 children.

Given the testimony of Spotswood's dealings with other tribes, it is most likely that those 41 student hostages lived in the Saponie Town.[29] As we consider the Indian School and its students, we should understand the multiple demands it must have placed on a town numbering only 300 men, women, and children. No written records exist that describe where these children slept, nor do we know how they were fed and otherwise cared for. Perhaps their shelter was the "handsome school" that Griffin mentioned. But that sort of structure alone seems inadequate for 41 children. Given the resources at Christanna, it is clear that the responsibility for the care of the student hostages at the Indian School fell on the Saponie Town, and it fell especially on the women of the town, whose gender-specific responsibilities were, among other things, to supervise young children, maintain the houses, weave mats for bedding, harvest and gather food, and prepare meals. Future archaeological evidence will provide a better understanding of life at the Saponie Town, but even in the absence of that, it is clear that the educational and religious initiatives at Christanna came at a cost beyond the expense of the school house and Griffin's salary. The responsibility of hosting foreign tribal students at the

Indian School was carried on the backs of the women of *Chunkete Posse*.

Chapter Seven

Attacks on the Fort

The first recorded assault on Fort Christanna was not an attack by any Indian tribe. It was a political attack that came at the hand of Englishmen and the Virginia House of Burgesses, and it was directed in large part against Governor Spotswood. It resulted in the disallowance of funds for the Fort, and in the eventual English departure from Christanna.

Whatever else Fort Christanna may have been, in 1714 it was a new development in Virginia's trading economy. The Fort at Christanna was conceived as the central trading outpost, or "factory," for the Virginia Indian Company's monopolistic fur trade south of the James River. Spotswood had advanced the idea of this trade monopoly in order to improve the efficiency of the peltry trade and to correct the difficulties created by the behavior of unscrupulous independent traders.[1] The monopoly, as the Governor laid it out, would cut down on unfair trade practices with Indians, and would put an end to trade-related conflicts with the government in South Carolina. There were multiple aspects to

Attacks on the Fort

Spotswood's "Act for the Better Regulation of the Indian Trade," including Indian education and the defense of the colony, but at the heart of Spotswood's reforms was profit-making.

In both England and Virginia, the idea of the Indian Company's monopoly raised the ire of those who advocated free trade. English merchants and Virginia traders who previously had made profits as middlemen soon found themselves cut out of the fur trade. Some who had already shipped English goods to America for exchange through their independent traders were left with the dilemma of having to ship their goods back home or sell them to the monopoly. Resentment toward the Governor grew on both sides of the Atlantic in reaction to the new trade regulations. The reforms related to Christanna were viewed by some as profiteering after it was revealed that Spotswood had not only invested in the Indian Company at the highest level allowed, but that he may have invested further under the name of his housekeeper. Through all of this, Spotswood defended what had been accomplished, and insisted that investment in the trade monopoly was always open to all, including the Indians at the schools. In the end those in London who were against the Act and the monopoly prevailed because these were seen as restraints on trade. Furthermore, these were viewed as being in direct contradiction to instructions given to the Royal Governor.[2] The Indian Act of 1714 was repealed on July 31, 1717.[3] With that, funding for the Governor's work at Christanna was disallowed. The political axe had fallen on Fort Christanna.

English involvement at Christanna did not end immediately after the disallowance, however. In order to protect the Tributaries at the Fort, to provide defense from tribal incursions, and to maintain good relations newly established with the Catawba and their allied towns, the Virginia Council requested that the Indian Company continue to maintain the guard, the hostages, and the fortifications at Christanna. The Council also called on the Company to continue the trade.[4]

For the colonial English, though, the fate of the Fort was sealed. The House of Burgesses refused to acknowledge there was a defensive need for the Fort, or that circumstances required any regulation of trade. They voted for the return of the Catawba hostages unless the newly empowered independent traders were willing to support them.[5] They regarded the project of Tributary Indian settlements set forth in the Treaties of 1713/14 a failure, since only the Saponie Tributaries had complied. And for that reason the Burgesses saw no need to continue funding the Fort. In the end the Company was never reimbursed for their expenditures there.[6]

In the period following the loss of support from London and from the Burgesses, Fort Christanna continued to play an important role in trade and Indian relations. It remained an important trading center for the Virginia Indian Company that continued their trade in competition with private traders.[7] As late as 1721, after the demise of the Virginia Indian Company, the Virginia Council gave diplomatic gifts to Chickasaw and Cherokee trading parties in Williamsburg and invited them to trade at Fort Christanna. It was ordered "that there be presented to each of the Great Men of the Chickasaw and Chirokee Indians now here, One Trading Gun, or Fuzil, and as much powder and Shott as they shall have occasion for in their Journey home, and that the same be

Attacks on the Fort

delivered them at Christanna."[8] The Fort continued to be a place preferred by certain tribes for treaty making, as well. In May of 1723, the Tributary Tribes "South of the James River" requested representation from the colonial government as they developed a preliminary "Treaty of peace and friendship" with the Tuscarora, and the preferred location for the talks was Christanna.[9]

The threat of violence grew at Fort Christanna in the months immediately following the disallowance. Late in the summer of 1718 it came to a head. Spotswood reported to the Board of Trade that in August, Five Nations and Tuscarora Indians had committed a murder at a remote Virginia plantation, and that plans for another attack were thwarted near the North Carolina Governor's house. Even more troubling, though, was the news that "Northern Indians" had come to Fort Christanna and had demanded of Captain Hix that the Saponie Tributaries "be delivered up to them." Spotswood told the Lords of Trade that, though funding for the guard and the repair of the Fort had been cut off, he could not leave the only fully co-operative Tributary Nation defenseless.[10] He felt compelled to act: "And, therefore, I removed them all into the Fort, w'ch the Late Indian Comp'ny, after their Dissolution, at the desire of the Gov't here, had rebuilt, and made of sufficient strength to baffle any enemy."[11] In his support of the loyal Saponie Tribes, Spotswood again inserted himself into the ancient blood feud, and this time he had clearly involved the Fort.

Realizing the futility of attacking Fort Christanna, the Northern Indians offered terms of peace to their ancient enemies, the Saponie, and departed. The urge to blood vengeance would not be so easily extinguished, however. Peace at the Fort would not last. Less than a year later, in

July 1719, the intertribal violence resumed at Christanna. Warriors from the Five Nations were involved with the destruction of the Saponie cornfields at *Chunkete Posse*, just downhill from the Fort. The Saponie living in the Fort raced out of the gate, and a firefight ensued. In response, Spotswood complained to Col. Schuyler, President of the Council of New York, that two Saponie were killed in this breach of the peace, as well as four Northern Indians. In the same letter that enumerated a litany of problems with the Northern Indians, Spotswood reported furiously that in September of that year, Iroquoian warriors from the Five Nations "lay in ambush before the gate of the fort" through the night and shot the first Saponie who left the Fort in the morning. He wrote that the Northern Indians and their allies continued shooting at the Fort until the English who were within fired the 1400-pound cannon in defense.[12] Retaliatory violence among tribes had reached a new level, and Fort Christanna, itself, was being fired upon.

Additional details related to the attack on the Fort emerged on July 14 and later on December 10 when Nottoway and Meherrin Indians came before the Governor and the Council, accompanied by a band of six Onondaga, a Five Nations tribe. At these Council meetings the Iroquoian-speaking Tributaries were pursuing an accusation that young Saponie men had killed and scalped a young Nottoway man. In the course of the questioning, the Indians admitted that eight Nottoways and twelve Meherrins had been involved with the ambush on the Saponies at the Fort, and that they were joined in the attack by Senecas (Five Nations) and Tuscaroras.[13]

Council records related to this matter reflect the intersection of two forms of justice. One form was the current English system of calling for witnesses – Native and English – to give testimony and evidence that would lead to a verdict and, if deserved, a penalty defined by both custom and written law.[14] An *individual* would be found guilty or liable, or not. Justice was tied to the responsibility of a person. The other form was the age-old indigenous code of justice – the law of equivalent retaliation or *lex talionis*. For all the Tributary Tribes, an offence committed deserved a similar offence in response.[15] In this form of justice the response was not typically to the offending individual. Response to an offense was *tribal*.

Both approaches to justice were in play in the series of Council sessions that were in many ways a kind of trial for the Indians involved. In Williamsburg the Governor and the Council pursued responsibility for the murder of the Nottoway man by seeking witnesses who were difficult to find. The Saponie were half-hearted in their co-operation, and neither they nor the Tuscarora attended the final session. By the time the Council considered the offense, the Nottoway and the Meherrin and their Iroquoian-speaking brothers from other tribes had already dealt out justice in the traditional way. Their tribal response to the offense by the Saponie had called for a reciprocal attack on the Saponie. There was no need to wait for December 8, the date originally set by the Virginia Council to hear witnesses. In response to the June murder, Nottoway justice was delivered to the Saponie in September in the form of gunfire on the Fort.

It is reasonable to think that the murder in June of the Nottoway man, and the Saponie's subsequent public display of his scalp precipitated the retaliatory cornfield attack by the Nottoway's Iroquoian allies. The retaliation was well planned. Sometime before September 4, 1719, the Commissioner for Indian Affairs in Albany reported to Spotswood that an Indian Headman from Virginia had come north to ask the Five Nations to "fall on the Indians settled at Christanna," and the Headman offered them sufficient powder and lead shot for that purpose.[16] Apparently, the Iroquois agreed to this request.

In pursuit of a peace, on December 9 Spotswood called the Iroquoian-speaking Headmen to appear before Council. They presented themselves at Council with an Onondaga Headman, *Connaughtoorah,* and five other Northern warriors. The Governor negotiated with *Connaughtoorah,* but the Onondaga leader refused to agree to a peace with the Saponie. His only concession was a pledge not to attack the Saponie Tributaries in the English settlements or within 20 miles of Fort Christanna. According to the agreement, both parties "were at Liberty to attack each other" at any other place.[17] The Council concluded the agreement with the promise of a belt of *wampum* for *Connaughtoorah* to carry back to the Five Nations as a token of peace. Additional diplomatic gifts included a Stroudwater trade blanket for each of the Northern warriors present and a laced hat for both the Onondaga leader and his interpreter.

CHAPTER EIGHT

Dissatisfaction and Departure

By the end of the year 1719, the region surrounding Christanna and the Fort had become a dangerous and unsettled place. The circumstance of the Saponie was changing. They were living in the Fort for protection, but in December they failed to come before the Council in Williamsburg as they had been directed.[1] In April 1720 they did not deliver to the Governor the required tribute of three arrows and still had not done so by October.[2] Their reasons were never recorded. It may have been a response to the danger of travel in the region because of frequent intertribal hostilities. It may have been a tribal statement to the English who had cut off funds to Fort Christanna, affecting the guard and needed repairs. It may have been related to resentment following the demise of the Virginia Indian Company, effectively sidelining the Tributaries and reducing the benefits they were accustomed to. We do not know, but any or all of these could have been the cause. Given what we know about the important Native traditions of diplomatic gift giving, the failure to present the gift arrows was certainly a slight, and it clearly signaled a severance in the relationship with the English. Things had become different for the Saponie at Christanna.

The continuing hostilities between the Saponie Tributaries and the Five Nations brought new developments beginning in 1720. Situated in the dangerous mid-Atlantic region between New York and Virginia, tribes from Pennsylvania – the Connestogo (Susquehannock), Showanoe (Shawnee), and Ganowass (Piscataway), each under the protection of the Five Nations – came to Williamsburg in November to make a treaty of friendship with the Christanna Indians.[3] In October of the following year deputies from the Five Nations came to Council, recounting "former injuries done by the Totteros" and "desiring liberty to cutt off the said Tottero Indians."[4] The resolution for each of these situations was agreement to affirm that the Potomac River and the Great Mountains to the west (Blue Ridge) would be boundary lines between the Nations that no tribe would cross. This would be formalized eventually at Albany in 1722 with the *Great Treaty*.

Chickasaw and Cherokee delegations came to Williamsburg in 1721 with concerns about traders in their region far to the west, following the demise of the Virginia Indian Company. The Council minutes highlight the problems of these western tribes:

> The Factors [traders] for the late Indian Company who have hitherto continued to Trade among the Chirokees and other Southern Indians are returned home and withdrawn their Effects, as not finding sufficient Encouragement for continuing that Commerce.[5]

Dissatisfaction and Departure

The Council conveyed to the delegations that tribal conflicts in the west were causing the traders to withdraw. They assured the delegations that trade would continue, however, and that Fort Christanna would remain open to them for powder and shot.

The playing field had changed dramatically for the Saponie. The Governor and Council in Williamsburg were presenting gifts to new tribes and even to enemies of the Tributaries. The Catawba were reportedly becoming a dubious ally. In 1727 a report came to the Virginia Council informing them that the Catawba were robbing and threatening the English inhabitants on the Roanoke River. The report went on to say it was expected that:

> ...They would return soon with a more considerable number and do more mischief, not only to the English Inhabitants, but to the Tributary Indians; and that there was some reason from their insolent behaviour of late, to apprehend they design'd to take possession of Christanna Fort, in which there are several Cattabaws at this time..."[6]

A sequence of intertribal revenge killings followed in 1728, involving the Tottero, Nottoway, Tuscarora, Catawba, and Saponie, creating ongoing turmoil that drew in the English. Several of the Saponie threatened war and attacks on the English over the imprisonment of three of their Headmen, Harry Irwin, Tom, and *Pyor*, related to the killing of two of the Nottoway.[7] The son of the "Totero King" was killed in an apparent retributive attack by a Nottoway man. Subsequent to that, the Tottero Headman threatened the lives of the Governor and others, and orders were issued for his imprisonment.[8] In December a hunting party of Saponie was suspected of killing a colonist, and Virginia's

Governor William Gooch dispatched Capt. Henry Embry and 37 Surry County militiamen to find and confront them.[9] By the end of the year, the Saponie Tributaries were ready to leave Virginia. The English and their Governor were no longer reliable allies.

In the spring of 1729 Governor Gooch received word that the Saponie did not plant their cornfields. He realized what that meant – their departure was imminent.[10] In the summer a respected Saponie Headman who was intoxicated killed a colonist. The Headman was willingly delivered by the Saponie to be tried for the crime. Saponie leaders argued that the defendant should not be held responsible for what he did "while deprived of his reason." He was found guilty, however, and was hanged.[11] It was soon after this execution that the Saponie Tributaries departed *Chunkete Posse* and Fort Christanna. Sometime before October they moved south to live again among the Catawba towns.[12]

Underlying the conflict created by the execution of the Saponie Headman in 1729 was the ongoing impact of alcohol on the tribe. Thirteen years before this event Spotswood had written to the Lords Commissioners of Trade regarding unscrupulous traders at English plantations who gave Indians alcohol to take advantage of them in trading deerskins.[13] This practice resulted in unsettling violent reprisals on the part of the Indians. Spotswood reported the following year that in response to alcohol-related abuses, "the Indians, being unacquainted with the methods of obtaining reparation by Law, frequently revenged themselves by the murder of the persons who thus treated them, or, (according to their notions of Satisfaction,) of the next Englishman

Dissatisfaction and Departure

they could most easily cutt off."[14] It was not only in trade that the English took advantage of Indians under the influence of alcohol. On April 26, 1727, two years before the Headman's execution, Saponie leaders came before the Virginia Council to complain that "one John Prowse of Hannover County being sometime ago at a horse-race on Maherine River" set fire to a Saponie Indian who was "very much in drink" and asleep. The Saponie man died from his injuries a few days later. On that same day, Saponie Headmen attempted to deal with a particular source of the alcohol problem by delivering before the Virginia Council a complaint about a trader, Martin Lyon, who "frequently brings Rum into their town, and sells the same to their young men whereby great disorders are committed among them."[15] Tribal leaders recognized that rum brought destruction and chaos to *Chunkete Posse*. No doubt the impact of alcohol on their people forced the Headmen to question the value of their continued interaction with the English.

The contemporary commentator, William Byrd II, attributed the setbacks and departure of the Christanna Indians to the influence of alcohol. In his *History of the Dividing Line*, he offered his compressed overview of what had transpired with the Saponie Tribes at Christanna:

> Colonel Spotswood, our then lieutenant governor, having a good opinion of their fidelity and courage, settled them at Christanna, ten miles north of Roanoke, upon the belief that they would be a good barrier, on that side of the country, against the incursion of all foreign Indians. And in earnest they would have served well enough for that purpose, if the white people in the neighbourhood had not debauched their morals, and ruined their health with rum, which was the cause of many disorders,

and ended at last in a barbarous murder committed by one of these Indians when he was drunk, for which the poor wretch was executed when he was sober...The Sapponies took this execution so much to heart, that they soon after quitted their settlement and removed in a body to the Catawbas.[16]

Alcohol was an important but unwritten item on the Indian traders' list of European goods for exchange. Rum brought with it tribal disruption, conflict, violence, and health problems. Alcohol came as a new plague to all Southeastern Indian tribes, and the Christanna Indians were not spared its effects.

In 1730, a year after the Saponie Tributaries departed their tract of land, it was parceled out through patents to several Englishmen. The 23,040 acre tract was divided among a group of Virginia's elite – 6000 acres to Henry Harrison, 12,000 acres to John & Joseph Allen, 1200 acres to Thomas Cock, and 2000 acres each to Thomas Ravenscroft and Benjamin Edwards.[17] An amount was allocated for stockholders in the Virginia Indian Company, as compensation for their losses, but the acreage assigned to other owners, in fact, exceeded the original 23,040 acres. It seems that no Indian Company investor ever claimed a part of the land.

The men who petitioned for patents to Christanna land knew the value of land near Indian towns and trading centers. As early as November of 1719, men of the Harrison and Edwards families petitioned for 6000 acres lying on both sides of the Roanoke River where an important Indian trading path crossed it.[18] In May of 1720, Henry Harrison, Nathaniel Harrison, John Allen, and William Edwards had petitioned for 3000 acres on the Roanoke from "the Totero King's house" to Canoe

Dissatisfaction and Departure

Creek.[19] In 1728 Benjamin Edwards had attempted to acquire 2000 acres of the Saponie tract that was associated with the defunct Virginia Indian Company, but the petition was rejected.[20] The record is clear that even before the Saponie Land tract was parceled out, these land speculators had acquired sizable parcels surrounding the Indian Tract. They knew that land near an Indian trading center delivered profits. Doubtless, the new owners of the land at Fort Christanna and *Chunkete Posse*, encouraged continued Indian trade there.

It was not only the English who saw a new opportunity in the Saponie Tribes' departure. Other Indian tribes had grown to depend on the trade at Christanna. In the vacuum created by the Saponie move, the Catawba were quick to act. In October 1729 they relayed through traders a message to the Council of Virginia that they desired a treaty of Friendship with Virginia.[21] Just as it was for the new English owners of Christanna land, their clear tribal intent was to secure a foothold for a beneficial trading relationship.

By 1732 the Saponie departed from the Catawba villages that increasingly had become an amalgamation of many refugee tribes from various regions.[22] We do not know the reasons for their departure, but intense competition for trade goods among the many Catawba tribes and the continued predations of the Northern Iroquois must have forced the decision. The Saponie returned to Virginia in that year with new kin and allies, the Saraw, and they petitioned Governor Gooch and the Council for a place in Virginia they could settle together.

> Divers of the Sapony Indians being return'd into this Colony from the Cattabaws this day attended the Gov r & in behalf of their Nation desir'd that they

> may have leave to settle again under the protection of this Government intimating also that the Saraw Indians are willing to cohabit with them and it is thereupon resolv'd That Leave be granted the sd Sapony Indians to return into this Colony with such of the Saraws as shall think fit to incorporate with them & to seat themselves on any Lands they shall chuse not being already granted to any of his Majesty's Subjects either on the River Roanoke or Appamatox & that upon their notifying to the Governor the place they shall chuse a Tract of Land be laid out for them equal to that they formerly held at Christanna.[23]

The alliance of the Saraw with the Saponie Tribes was advantageous for both groups. The Saraw had long pursued a formalized relationship with Virginia. In the wake of conflicts with South Carolinians, they had looked northward to Virginia for access to European trade goods. From July 1715 to February 1715/1716, Saraw delegations had traveled three times to Williamsburg to establish relations with Virginia, with a goal of moving closer to the colony.[24] In 1717 they traveled with the Catawba to deliver their hostage children to Fort Christanna, as the Governor had required.[25] The 1732 incorporation with the Tributary Saponie Tribes was politically wise for the Saraw, as it facilitated a renewed relationship with Virginia under a new Governor. Furthermore, the new alliance strengthened the military capabilities of both of these relatively small tribal groups.

Beyond this, however, both tribal groups had a need for their villages to have a sufficient number of marriageable individuals of childbearing age. Under constant assault from enemies and European diseases, tribal numbers for both groups were reduced. The Saponie decision to settle with the Saraw may be viewed as a tribally initiated

Dissatisfaction and Departure

choice to ensure a sustainable population. The same sort of choice may be seen in earlier Saponie circumstances. This reality may have been at play in the connections between earlier towns: Sapon and Pintahae (Lederer,1670), "Sapiney Indian Town" and "Saponeys West," (Batts and Fallam, 1671), the Occoneechee, Tottero, and Saponie Islands in the Roanoke (Alvord and Bidgood, 1674; also Byrd), Toteros, Saponas, and Keyauwees preparing to join together on the Yadkin (Lawson, 1701), Saponie, Occoneechee, Stukanox, and Tottero settling together at *Unotee* and later at *Chunkete Posse* (1708-13; 1714-1729). Just as it made sense for larger tribal groups such as the Catawba and the Five Nations to incorporate outsider tribes in order to strengthen themselves and compensate for population losses, it made even more sense for smaller tribes and bands to do this. Combined and paired settlements may also have related to kinship matters and exogamous marriage patterns, both of which were important to indigenous peoples. The Saraw and the Saponie shared a common language and region, and that commonality brought with it shared societal and cultural practices.[26] There is scant documented evidence for kinship patterns among Eastern Siouan tribes, but an interpretation of the Saponie-Saraw alliance that recognizes kinship and population necessities is a reasonable thing to consider.[27]

The Saponie Tribes, now with their Saraw brothers, returned to a Virginia with fewer opportunities for them. By 1732 Virginia had become a colony where the defensive need for Tributary Tribes had diminished and where Indian trade patterns had come to involve competing tribes to the west.[28] Aware of a weakened alliance with Anglo-Virginians, in 1733 the Saponie

Tribes boldly moved to build relationships with the Iroquoian tribes to the south and east. In the spring the Saponie petitioned Tom Blunt, the leader of the Upper Tuscarora, to allow them to be received as friends and to reside in the Tuscarora town, *Reskooteh*. On April 3, 1733, North Carolina's Governor Burrington and his Council gave Blunt permission to allow the Saponie Tribes to join with them.[29] Three months later the Saponie petitioned Governor Gooch of Virginia for permission to make a treaty with the Tuscarora and to incorporate with them in their town. Permission to do so was granted. Governor Gooch, however, reiterated his earlier offer of a tract of land apart from the English settlements between the Roanoke and Appomattox Rivers. Gooch sent Robert Hix, the old trader and former captain of the rangers at Fort Christanna, to oversee the treaty with the Tuscarora.[30] At the same time, subsequent to a period of violent attacks and reprisals following the Saponie return to Virginia, the Saponie and the Nottoway agreed before the Virginia Council to put an end to their hostilities. This removed a major obstacle to a stable alliance with the Upper Tuscarora. Given the sequence of determined negotiations in 1733, it seems likely that the Tribes once known as Christanna Indians moved to live among people in the Upper Tuscarora villages, along the lower Roanoke River in what is present day Bertie County, North Carolina.

The relocation was not a complete one, or it was not lasting, however. A record from 1737 that mentions "Sappone Indians cabbins" in Amelia County, Virginia (now Nottoway County).[31] Situated just east of the present-day town of Crewe, Virginia, these "Sappone cabins" suggest that at least some Saponie did choose to

Dissatisfaction and Departure 109

settle on land between the Appomattox and Roanoke Rivers – land that Governor Gooch had offered them.

It is clear from the archaeological record that activity at Fort Christanna continued past the Saponie's 1729 departure. Fragments of European trade pipes that were excavated at the fort site in the 1979 season of Mary Beaudry's archaeological work there have been reliably dated. These fragments were taken from the bastion house areas, and along the fort walls. The "mean date" of the pipe fragments analyzed from the first extensive excavation of the fort was 1741. Taken as a whole, 80% of the pipe fragments were from 1710-1750, and 14% of the pipe fragments were classified as being from the 1750-1800 range.[32] Pipestem dating that includes the later excavations led by Christopher Stevenson produced comparable dates. With the additional pipestem fragments from his excavation of bastion houses, wall sections, an interior structure, and an exterior location, the sample of 648 items had 80% from 1710-1750, and 11% from 1750-1800. These data are a clear indication that activity at the Fort continued even past mid-century.[33] It is likely that the Saponie Tribes who returned to Virginia to benefit from trade would have been among the Indian participants in the ongoing trade at the Fort. Beyond this, evidence regarding the use of Fort Christanna vanishes. Within a few generations the place was remembered only vaguely on maps and in local folklore as Fort Hill, awaiting its eventual rediscovery by archaeologists more than two centuries later.

CHAPTER NINE

Persistence of Traditions

The Indians were awash with change at *Chunkete Posse*, and many tribal traditions were challenged at that place. Cultural change for the Saponie Tribes did not begin with the arrival of Spotswood and the Indian School, however. Before Christanna, throughout the region European firearms had become the principle implements for Siouan hunters and warriors.[1] By 1716, at Christanna, the bow and arrow was a weapon only for boys.[2] European trade blankets had replaced dressed deerskins for clothing. Both Lawson and Hugh Jones observed an indigenous pictographic writing system that hunters and others used to communicate with each other, but this practice was soon lost in the chaos of the time.[3]

Many distinctly Saponie traditions persisted, however. The efforts to suppress traditional religion at the Indian School, for example, were not entirely successful. Ned Bear-skin's conversations with Byrd are clear evidence of that. His belief in the Saponie Creator, in the Spirit of the Woods, and in traditional cosmology survived the English instruction that sought to contradict those beliefs. Hugh Jones commented on the students educated in the Indian Schools, saying that, "Some indeed, after seeming Conversion have apostatized and returned to their own Ways, chiefly because they can live with less Labour, and more Pleasure and Plenty as *Indians,* than they can with us."[4] And William Byrd wrote, "After they return'd home, instead of civilizeing and converting the rest, they have immediately Relapt into Infidelity and Barbarism themselves."[5] Traditional Saponie religious beliefs persisted, and in new, adapted ways. Bear-skin used a new language to tell Byrd of the old Saponie beliefs he held. It is likely that the Saponie hunter, still living at Christanna, learned his English just 12 years earlier through the Indian School.

Though the Saponie transition to the use of doglock and flintlock muskets was nearly complete by 1700, the Tributaries had a particular traditional way of hunting that continued for decades after their Christanna experience. Firehunting was a common Saponie technique for killing game.[6] Jones and Byrd were both aware of Saponie firehunting.[7] Lawson described the practice:

> When these Savages go a hunting, they commonly go out in great Numbers, and oftentimes a great many Days Journey from home, beginning at the coming in of the Winter; that is, when the Leaves are fallen from the Trees, and are become dry. 'Tis then they burn the Woods, by setting Fire to the Leaves, and wither'd Bent and Grass... Thus they go and fire the Woods for many Miles, and drive the Deer and other Game into small Necks of Land and Isthmus's, where they kill and destroy what they please.[8]

In 1740 a colonist, William Bohannon, went to court in Orange County, Virginia to complain that his pigs were being killed. Under oath he testified that, "about twenty six Saponey Indians who inhabited Col. Spotswood's land in Fox's Neck ... go about and do a great deal of mischief by setting fire to the woods, and more especially on the 20 day of last April, when two farrows of pigs were burnt in their beds."[9] What was regarded by Bohannon as mischief was a continuation of the Saponie firehunting tradition. Two years later, in January 1742/43, ten Saponie Indians were brought to Orange County Court for hog stealing and burning the woods. These hunters clearly had a past connection with Christanna – not only had they been living on Alexander Spotswood's land, but one of the Indians was named "Charles Griffin," apparently having taken the name of the School-Master.[10] These court records are snapshots of the continuing Saponie hunting tradition.

Traditional political structures among the Tributary Tribes endured for some time, as well. Though Spotswood and his government came to refer to these tribes collectively as one Nation, the Saponie,[11] in 1720 the Governor drafted a treaty that listed the Tributary Tribes separately as "Saponie Tottero Stukanox Occonechee Indians."[12] And in 1722 at the Albany Council, in speaking with the Northern Indians, he stated "the Christanna Indians whom you call Todirichroones... we comprehend under the name, the Saponies, Ochineeches, Stenkenocks, Meipontskys and Toteroes...."[13] All along, even though living together, the tribes apparently maintained their separate political identities. In 1716, John Fontaine had, perhaps, expected a "King" of the Saponie to come and parley with the Governor, but 12 elders came instead. Unknown to Fontaine, apparently the "Kings" and the Headmen from each of the Tributary Siouan Tribes had come as a group to talk. Even though the tribes were settled together in a single town, their separate forms of tribal leadership apparently persisted. Evidence of that is scattered through the Council records. In 1727 the "Occaneeche King" is mentioned in Council in connection with a Catawba and Saponie attack on the Nottoway.[14] Council minutes for August 16, 1728 report that the "Totero King" came to complain that the Nottoway killed his son. Living together as allies, the Tributaries maintained their separate traditions of tribal rule. What Spotswood said of the Christanna Indians at the outset remained true. He had "engaged the Saponie, Oconeechee, Stuckanox and Tottero Indians, (being a people speaking much the same language, and therefore confederated together, *tho' still preserving their different Rules*) [italics mine]"[15]

In the mid-1700s, as the Saponie migrated, continued to assimilate, and developed various new strategies for survival, references to the traditional tribal names began to fade away. Even in the midst of these great transitions, though, we can see the continuity of their tribal identity and political structures. For the period following the return of the Saponie Tribes to Virginia in 1732, the Tottero are the best documented of the tribes that had resided at *Chunkete Posse,* and their history makes this point clearly.

William Byrd II was in error in his *Dividing Line* manuscript (1728) in reporting, as he did, the death of the "Tetero King." According to Byrd, he was "the last Man of his Race and Nation," leaving behind only a daughter who committed suicide two years later.[16] In fact, the so-called "King" of the Tottero people was still petitioning the Virginia Council in the year Byrd was writing his account.[17] The Tottero people (who came to be known north of Virginia as the "Tutelo") and some of the other Siouan Tributaries adapted to circumstances in Virginia by migrating north to Pennsylvania, settling on the eastern branch of the Susquehanna River at Shamokin and then Skogari (Catawissa Creek). By 1753 a body of "*Todarighroones*" – a general Iroquoian term meaning, at that time, "Christanna Indians" – was adopted into the League of the Iroquois by the Cayuga.[18] In doing that, the League of the Iroquois (*Haudenosaunee*), that included the Five Nations tribes and the recently incorporated Lower Tuscarora, became their protectors. Later, the Tutelo and those Saponie and Occoneechee who were with them moved farther north as a result of the French and Indian War, and they would eventually settle among the Cayuga people. Colonial armed forces destroyed the Cayuga main village in 1779, and soon after, the Saponie and Occoneechee apparently split off from the Tutelo.[19] The Tutelo moved to Ontario with the Cayuga who were loyal to England. A treaty from 1789 indicates a remnant band of some Saponie may have settled at the Cayuga reservation on the Seneca River in New York.[20] Tottero-Tutelo political structure adapted with continuity over time. Though tribal numbers declined as a result of conflicts, relocations, intermarriage, and disease, the Tutelo chief played a role within the Iroquois League until 1953.[21]

Spotswood described the Tributary Tribes at Christanna as "a people speaking much the same language," so the study of any of their language that survived is a window into the cultures of all of those tribes.[22] Most of what is known of the language spoken by the Siouan Tributaries comes from the study of the Tutelo language as it persisted as a spoken Indian language until at least 1898. Vocabularies of the Tutelo language were still being collected as late as 1913, and tribal members were able to interpret the words to surviving Tutelo songs forty years after that.[23] Living among the Cayuga, the Tutelo continued to preserve and perform important ceremonial Tutelo songs, all tied through language and ceremony to their Eastern Siouan origins. Those continuing rites included the Harvest, Spirit Adoption, Spirit Release, and Bear ceremonies. Recognizing the power in them, the Iroquois adopted and performed those Eastern Siouan ceremonies, and some Tutelo songs are still performed in 2018.[24] Both the Tutelo people and their rituals merged with the Cayuga, and in that way their tribal legacy has lived on through the culture of their former Northern enemies. Tottero-Tutelo history is the embodiment of a kind of endurance that William Byrd II could not have imagined.

Less of the language spoken by the Tributaries remained in the South, though it once was regionally important. In April of 1728 it was the recommendation of the Virginia Council that the salary of the interpreter to the Saponie, Charles Kimball, be increased to 4000 pounds of tobacco per year, so the tribal language must have been regarded as important for diplomacy.[25] In the same year, William Byrd thought it necessary to take Kimball with the dividing line surveyors' party. Byrd's choice of the Saponie interpreter indicates is that, at that time, there must have been many speakers of the Siouan language in the Piedmont region.[26] Only a few Saponie names and words survived in the Saponie's southern homeland. In Brunswick County, Virginia variations of the place name "*Chunkete Posse*" (*Junckatapurse*) persisted until 1792 in

Road Orders and Vestry Book minutes. To the west in Person County, NC, Hyco River and Hyco Lake were named with a truncated form of *Hicootomoni*, meaning Turkey Buzzard Creek, after the great bird regarded as sacred by many Southeastern tribes. Near the site of the Fort Christanna, "Totaro Creek" and "Genito Creek," are features that preserve Saponie words and history. Other than these few words of Indian origin and a hand-full of others on old maps, a living language in the south did not last. The Saponie language in the south survived in English language manuscripts: John Fontaine's *Journal*, William Byrd's *Dividing Line Histories*, and Alexander Irvine's *Field Book*.

Family stories from a modern tribal group, the Occaneechi Band of the Saponi Nation, tell of a Mr. G. C. Whitmore from Alamance County, NC, who at age 97 recalled that his grandfather, Andrew Whitmore, spoke in a language that was not English, and that the elder man would translate the meaning for his grandson. Unfortunately none of these words were written down, and none entered into memory. Whether this was a survival of the Eastern Siouan language will never be known.[27]

Though the Eastern Siouan language shared by the Christanna Tributaries eventually was overwhelmed in Virginia and North Carolina, it is clear that the Indian people endured in their southern homelands. We recall that in 1740, 26 Saponie men were mentioned in Orange County, Virginia as living on Alexander Spotswood's land. It is reasonable to think they lived there with families. In 1755 Governor Dobbs of North Carolina reported that there were 28 "Saponas" residing in Granville County, NC on the border with Virginia. This information came to him in connection with a muster roll taken by Colonel William Eaton.[28] Later, two Saponie Headmen from the Virginia-Carolina border represented their people in a meeting with Virginia's Governor Dinwiddie in 1757, regarding a military matter.[29] Succeeding Dinwiddie as Governor was Francis Fauquier who, in 1763, attested that, in addition to Eastern Shore and Europeanized Pamunkey Indians, the Saponie and other tribes were in Virginia living in traditional ways. The Governor wrote, "There are some of the Nottoway, Meherrin, Tuscaroras, and Saponys" who "lead in great measure the lives of wild Indians."[30] In 1764, the Indian Superintendent for the South, John Stuart, reported that in Virginia the "Nottways" and "Saponys" together had 60 gun-men.[31] Though by the end of the last quarter of the eighteenth-century acculturation forced many cultural adaptations on the Saponie, James Adair could write in 1775 that the Southern Saponie still referred to themselves by their tribal name: "In Virginia, resides the remnant of an Indian tribe, who call themselves Sepóne."[32] According to Ruth Wetmore, in the decades that followed, those descendants of the Christanna Indians who remained in Virginia and North Carolina became an invisible people, and over the next 200 years lived "as many Indians did on the margins of the predominantly white society, often owning no land... their geographic and cultural isolation tended to exclude them from more than passing notice."[33] Increasingly taking on the ways of the dominant culture, tribal identity became less visible in the historical record. Descendants of the Tributary Siouan Tribes settled in recognizable communities along the southwestern trading routes, in the borderlands between Virginia and

North Carolina, and in places that had been earlier settlement locations.³⁴

Four recognized tribes have documented their ancestral connection to the community of Saponie Indians associated with Christanna. In North Carolina, the Haliwa-Saponi, the Sappony, the Occaneechi Band of the Saponi Nation, and in Virginia, the recently federally recognized Monacan Indian Nation have each endured in isolated and self-supporting communities as Indian people. It has been a struggle against great odds for these communities to survive as Indian tribes. Legislation has at times denied their identity as Indians, but it has at other times affirmed it. In the face of many obstacles, the construction of tribal schools and tribal churches has often been a key to enduring tribal identity. Recently, several of the tribes initiated Tutelo-Saponi language education programs in an attempt to bring back to life the Indian language heard at *Chunkete Posse* and Fort Christanna. A contemporary song, "*Mahk Jchi* (Heartbeat Drum Song)," with lyrics in Tutelo-Saponi, came into being as a result of this effort. The song and the album of the same name garnered national recognition and the music was featured in film scores and anthologies.³⁵ The success of the educational efforts is evident among at the tribes, as well. At tribal youth camps children and elders speak words and phrases in the old language. At powwows tribal leaders offer prayers, and singers around the drums again raise their voices in the Tutelo-Saponi language.

Chapter Ten

Two Women

If the accounts of Christanna and *Chunkete Posse* misdirect because of their Anglocentric cultural perspectives, they skew the history further because they are almost exclusively accounts of men's activities. In eighteenth-century Virginia, observations of women's lives – both English and Native – were rare. At that time, women's lives and activities in general were overshadowed by and regarded as secondary to the activities, priorities, and interactions of men. Consequently women's stories were mostly lost, obscured, or never recorded in documents of the period.

For Native people at Christanna, the women's stories of weaving, ceramics, kinship, political authority, and the ways of daily sustenance are nearly entirely absent. An English document may have recorded that warriors "ravaged our Indians' cornfields," but there is nothing recorded that describes the genius of seed development and food preservation that was women's work there, nothing that told of the way they cleared their fields, and nothing about women's seasonal plantings and gatherings of plants for food and medicines.¹ Byrd mentioned in his *Dividing Line Histories* that women made baskets and wove fabric for their skirts from silk grass, but he does not describe the work involved.² Nor do the period sources tell us about Siouan women's trading activities in contrast with those of the men. What historian Theda Perdue learned from her study of the Cherokee is that there were gendered differences in Native approaches to trade. Women in Indian towns traded food and baskets out of an agricultural economy, while men engaged in hunting and traded in hides with a commercial economic approach. Perdue recognized that women's trade ethic was one of co-operation, while that of men was more individualistic. Generally stated, "men sold" and "women shared." In Perdue's analysis, women's approach to trade was a more conservative approach than that taken by men, and women's exchange adhered more closely to traditional tribal trading practices.³ What was true for the trading practices of Cherokee women was likely true for Siouan women, as well.

Byrd's *Dividing Line* account documents that four women came with a delegation of Saponie Headmen to visit him as he was leaving their territory, but nothing Byrd wrote speaks to the significance of the women at that meeting. He leaves us in the dark regarding the larger political influence women certainly held at their town, *Chunkete Posse*.⁴ Charles Griffin mentioned in his letter to the Bishop of London the kind reception given him at Christanna by the "Indian Queen, the great men, and, indeed, from all the Indians," but he provided no explanation for the apparent primacy he gave the Tributary Queen.⁵ Later, Griffin gave evidence in a deposition that the Governor afforded the Saponie

Queen greater respect than that given to the Headmen of the tribes. The School-Master reported that after the tribes relocated to Christanna, Spotswood gave the Queen (*Hoontkymiha*) two cows with calves, while giving the 12 Headmen only one cow with calf each.[6] In a letter Spotswood described a ten-year-old girl who died at the Christanna School as the "Queen of that nation," but nowhere are we told the tribal and political meaning of that Anglicized title of rank.[7] These references taken together, though, lead us to conclude that there was a social and political hierarchy at *Chunkete Posse*, and that, given the age of the child Queen, the role of Queen (*Hoontkymiha*) may have been an inherited one.

What we know about other Piedmont Siouan tribes amplifies our understanding of the political role of women at Christanna. When John Lawson visited the village of the Keyauwee in 1701, he met Keyauwee Jack, a Congaree Indian who had attained the status of "King" by marrying the "Queen" of the Keyauwee. Political leadership among the Keyauwee originated from a female, and her role as "Queen" (*Hoontkymiha*) was hereditary.[8] The Keyauwee were closely affiliated with the Saponie, Tottero, Occoneechee, and other Siouan tribal groups, and it is likely that these groups had similar matrilineal political systems. In addition to the "Queens" of the Saponie and the Keyauwee, we know from the signatories of the 1713/14 Treaty that the primary political leader of the Stukanoe was a *Hoontkymiha (Headwoman)*. All of this points to the considerable importance women must have had in political leadership at *Chunkete Posse*.

Despite the overwhelming male bias in the English records related to Fort Christanna, and their silence regarding the lives of women, two revealing stories of Native women were preserved – accounts of one woman from *Chunkete Posse* and another from Catawba. One tragic, the other almost redemptive, these stories together take us to the larger Indian experience at Christanna.

The Return of a Slave

On April 23, 1718, a complaint involving a Saponie woman who had been sold as a slave came before the Council of Virginia.[9] There is no record that tells us how this particular Saponie woman was taken prisoner, or what tribe had captured her and sold her as a slave. Like thousands of other Native people she was a victim of a cycle of violence that, at the time of Christanna, had become embedded in the fabric of Southeastern Indian cultures: Indians captured other Indians and sold them as slaves in order to acquire firearms, powder and shot; the muskets, powder and shot were needed for defense and for acts of reciprocal violence that included the taking of captives who, in turn, would be sold as slaves. Throughout the Southeast, all the tribes were caught in the cycle to some degree. Those tribes that did not sell slaves for muskets and powder were left unable to defend themselves and vulnerable to becoming slaves themselves. The tribal warrior culture of the Southeast to a great extent had become a slaving culture. The English with the access to guns, powder, and lead shot, encouraged the cycle and could manipulate tribes by providing trade goods and weapons, or not. Alongside the trade in pelts, the English trade in Indian slaves became, for a time, a primary and profitable enterprise.[10] Regular incursions of the Northern Tribes into the south worsened the situation. The attacks from the Five

Nations were primarily fed by the goal of taking captives to replenish lost tribal population due to diseases and warfare, and to avenge wrongs done to their people.[11] So this particular Saponie woman might have been captured by any of a number of enemy tribes. In the hearing before the Council of Virginia, it was only recorded that she was captured by "some Forreign Indians."

The Great Men of the Saponie came before the Council and told the woman's story. She had been bought as a slave by Nathaniel Malone. On learning the woman's circumstance, the Saponie made an arrangement to buy her freedom. Malone had set the price for the woman at 120 deerhides, roughly the cost of seven muskets. In terms of the exchange rates of the time, this was a typical price. Indian women and children were preferred over Indian men as slaves.[12] The Great Men told the Council they delivered 90 hides to Malone and planned to bring the remaining hides later. They went on to say that in the meantime, however, the Saponie woman, so close to regaining her freedom, fell ill and died. Hers was the fate of perhaps 80-90% of the North American Indian population who succumbed to the silent enemy of European diseases for which they had no immunities.[13]

The complaint before the Council was not about the fact that a Saponie woman had been captured, then sold as a slave. In 1718 the English purchase of an Indian slave was an ordinary matter. By Virginia law she was regarded as Nathaniel Malone's real estate. The matter before the Council was an effort by the tribe to recover the payment of deerhides they had made to Nathaniel Malone "for the Freedom of an Indian woman." The Englishman Malone came before the Council the next month and stated that the Saponie had given him only 74 skins toward her release before she died. In the end the Council decided that Malone should return 74 hides to the Saponie, rather than the 90 deer skins the Great Men claimed to have given him. The matter was settled. No one recorded the name of the woman from *Chunkete Posse*. She is only remembered as Nathaniel Malone's Saponie slave who died while she was in his service.

The Return of a Captive

There was no hint beforehand that anything dramatic was about to happen in the House of Burgesses on May 17, 1718. The first order of business came to the Assembly in the form of a communication from Governor Alexander Spotswood and the Council. It was a commonplace claim for reimbursement for a Ranger who had taken his troops to the head of the James River as inhabitants there had requested. So humdrum a request the first part was, there's no doubt the details were lost on some. The second item in the message, though, was of a different sort. It was a stunning story about a woman from the Catawba villages:

> The Governor and Council think fit to acquaint you that this Woman was taken Prisoner from *Christanna in April 1717* by the Northern Indians and carried to the *Mohacks* Country, and is the same which *Mr. Christopher Smith* was Sent to Albany to reclaim as it is mentioned in his transactions there now before your House After having made her escape from thence and layn upwards of five Months in the Woods she came in almost famished to a Plantation on the head of *James* River and was taken care of by the Claimant Her being made Prisoner while the Indians of her Nation were under the Protection of this Government made it necessary for the Government to take care of Sending her back to them and by that Act of Justice

and humanity the friendship of those Indians to this Government will undoubtedly be increased The Service which the Claimant did therein is therefore recommended to the consideration of your House.[14]

Of all the accounts related to Christanna, this stands almost alone with its happy ending. It is an epic story given to us with few details. The un-named woman was stolen at dawn from a foreign town and taken as a prisoner by the blood enemies of her people. Hers is a story of courage and endurance. A 500-mile journey of survival took her on a rough path between both English and Indians who would misunderstand her Siouan words. Either might have killed or enslaved her. Her astonishing return to find her people leaves us in awe of her strength, resourcefulness, and persistence. Her story was told in only three sentences that were written to justify a Ranger's compensation. Yet even in its brevity it is astonishing.

Later, Alexander Spotswood incorporated the details of the Catawba woman's compelling story in a letter he wrote to Governor Hunter of New York January 25, 1719/20. A portion of the letter briefly tells of a subsequent chapter in her life. In the year following her capture at Fort Christanna and subsequent escape and return, she was captured a second time by Five Nations warriors in an attack on a group of 140 Catawba in Carolina. Spotswood's admiration of her is almost palpable in his letter. He wrote, "[T]his very Woman was of that number of the one hundred & forty, and carried off captive again to the Northward, for she in 1718 made her Escape again, and came in a second time to me through Pensilvania and Maryland."[15]

Storytellers

These two stories were inadvertently preserved, embedded in a complaint about Indian policy and in proceedings related to reimbursement requests – a refund of deerskins and compensation for militia service. The women's lives were incidental to the matters at hand, and so the recorded details of the two women are scant. Taken together, though, the small stories of their circumstances magnify the larger story of the Indians at Christanna.

In the tragic details of her life, the Saponie woman who was Nathaniel Malone's slave gives voice to many other un-named Tributary Indians – the ones who were taken away by violence, the thousands who died of Old World diseases, and those who were enslaved and valued only in deerhides or European trade goods. Her brief story speaks of the injustices her people suffered at the hands of unscrupulous traders and English courts of law. But hers is not the only story.

There is also the account of the Catawba woman taken captive at Fort Christanna. In many ways hers is the story of those Indian people who somehow survived the chaos, diseases, and cultural disruptions that Europeans brought to their world. This anonymous Native woman traveled to Virginia from the Catawba villages and likely brought her son to the Indian School where he would remain a hostage. Twice she escaped captivity and traveled alone and on foot, without provisions, from New York to Virginia, then on to Carolina. Her epic struggle to survive speaks for the many bands of Indian people who persisted in spite of scarcity, dislocations, enslavement, and educational oppression. The account of the Catawba woman captured beside the English fort tells the story of those who have endured, as she did, to stay connected with kin and to maintain community *as Indian people*, even into the 21st century.

Overview

Understanding a Native Christanna

The Fort at Christanna attracted the full range of English and tribal engagement – political, economic, military, and cultural, but its function and significance evolved from 1714 to mid-century. It began as an outpost to defend a colony from Indian attack and ended with Indians taking shelter within it. The Fort was created to monopolize and regulate the regional Indian fur trade, but that would only last for the first four of its many years. The first documented attack it sustained came at the hands of Englishmen from Williamsburg and London, and that political attack would be its eventual undoing. Though formal English involvement diminished over time, the Fort continued on as an Indian place for trade and treaties well past the governorship of its originator, Alexander Spotswood. The changes that came to Fort Christanna are vivid testimony to a time of great turbulence and great transitions for Native peoples. A historical narrative of the Fort that includes accounts of the Native people engaged there not only enriches our understanding of the

Indians of the east, it also expands our understanding of the Virginia colony in the early-to-mid-eighteenth-century. The story of Christanna provides a distinct and corrective counterpoint to histories that have a focus on Anglocentric activities in the eastern parts of the colony. Christanna, the Fort, and the Saponie town draw our attention to a different Virginia whose activities and sources of meaning were centered in the west.

Fort Christanna was conceived and built at a time when cultures were colliding in the Southeast. Relentless militaristic forays from Northern tribes and their allies, attacks of slaving warriors from the South, the colonial expansion of the English, and the lure of European trade goods converged at Christanna. Situated as it was, in close proximity to traditionally important trading paths, and having a monopoly on the regional trade, the Fort was a crossroads for many Nations. In addition to the English, at least 23 tribes are recorded as trading, negotiating, making war, or concluding treaties at the Fort. Many tribes were coerced by circumstance and the English Governor to deliver children there to be re-educated and kept as hostages. The frontier where Christanna was situated was cultural, economic, and political, and that frontier faced both west and east. Cultural interaction changed the lives of the Virginia traders who frequented *Chunkete Posse* and other Indian towns, generating frontier moralities and lifeways that contrasted sharply with those in the rest of the colony.[1]

As the English advanced into the Piedmont region of Virginia and the Carolinas, a new world with global connections pressed in upon the traditional ways of the many tribes and villages of the region.[2] New technologies and great quantities of European goods upended the traditional lifeways and political structures of Indian peoples and redefined such core cultural components of their lives as warfare, hunting, political authority, languages, and societal roles. In many regions English profit motives transformed indigenous economies within a generation. For Indian peoples these developments were a mix of threat and opportunity.

The new opportunities came at a cost. Firearms made hunting easier, but they intensified intertribal violence and helped to transform the traditional approach to hunting into a commercial activity. The constant need for powder and shot required that all tribes establish and maintain trade relations with the same Europeans who were appropriating their traditional lands. The archaeological evidence at Fort Christanna reveals it to be a place where muskets were traded and repaired. Trade gun parts, abundant quantities of lead shot, a soapstone shot mold, and slag from a forge are testimony to the role the Fort played in this transition.[3]

By 1714 in the greater Southeast, given the new circumstances at every turn, the roles of indigenous men had shifted increasingly to the work of the warrior, the trader, and the hunter for hides, pelts, and prisoners to trade. The roles of Native women had changed in corresponding ways. The traditional domestic activities of women increasingly became work that supported the trade in European goods. Preparation of deerhides was work that formerly may have been shared by men and women, but at the time of Christanna it had become the exclusive work of women.[4] Archaeological evidence of thumb scrapers inside the Fort tells in a small way the story of the new work of Native women – they were not scraping, tanning, and smoking hides there for domestic clothing production. At Fort Christanna, women were processing hides for the trans-oceanic skin trade.

Symbolic of these social changes are several of the thumb scrapers excavated from the fort site: though the technique used to make the tools indicates Native manufacture, the scrapers were fashioned from pieces of broken wine bottles.[5] Green bottle glass blown in Europe had replaced the Indians' traditional regional chert, and it was being used by Native women in the Fort to process deerhides, eight of which could buy a new "Duffield blanket" from Europe. European trade blankets and trade cloth were status goods for Native people, and tribal preference for these new materials further diminished the traditional role of women as providers of fabric and clothing. Seemingly all things had become different. For the Indian people at Christanna, Europeans didn't discover a New World, they brought it with them to trade.

Christanna's history reveals how the success of the English colonies in many ways came at the expense of indigenous polities – tribes, chiefdoms, and nations – that, by intention or not, were fragmented, destroyed, or radically transformed by interactions with those who came from across the Atlantic. From the Native perspective, the English arrival and expansion in North America was an extended invasion and cultural assault. The new aggressor arrived with devastating new technologies and new diseases that cut into Native populations to an almost unimaginable degree. New things of beauty and power – trade goods from a global market — pried apart indigenous cultures from without and within. The English appetite for the land used by the tribes was insatiable. At Christanna, we can see how both education and religion were used by the English, in self-aware ways, to make tribes compliant with English intentions. At a certain level of analysis, then, the history of Fort Christanna is a series of documentary snapshots taken during the Anglo-European rise to complete economic and political domination over Indian tribes in Eastern North America.

From another perspective, however, the history of Fort Christanna tells the stories of Native groups in the process of improvising ways to survive in a difficult time. Among the many stories that come into view at Christanna, those of the confederated Saponie Tribes stand out most clearly. In comparison with other tribes who interacted at Christanna, the Siouan Tributaries' path to survival was a singular one. The way forward for this relatively small group of Siouan Indians involved a risky choice: the Saponie chose to form a close alliance with the ones who potentially were their most powerful adversaries, the English. In many ways their tribal approach was a successful one precisely because they were a relatively small group – a town of only 300. Tribal groups such as the Catawba or the Tuscarora, numbering in the thousands, posed a significant threat to the English.

The evolving Saponie strategy of survival, beginning with the Treaty of Middle Plantation, took advantage of their status as Tributary Indians. That strategy was manifest clearly at Christanna. The Saponie Tribes were the only Tributaries to participate fully in the Governor's resettlement project, as the Treaty of 1713/14 had required. They complied further by involving more than 70 of their children in the instruction at the Indian School. They assisted in the defense of the colony and surely must have helped construct the Christanna fort.

Overview: Understanding a Native Christanna 133

The tribal strategy for the Saponie Tributaries was to comply with the English in order to achieve tribal goals.

That firm alliance delivered the Saponie the protection they needed against their powerful, relentless, and well-armed Native enemies. The Saponie were militarily outmatched, outnumbered, and unable to provide for their own defense, but with the English as their ally, they were defended and provisioned. It was the Saponie's choice to seat their town "a musket shot away" from Fort Christanna. The proximity to the Governor's fort afforded them protection and, at the same time, gave them beneficial exchange rates at the place that had a trade monopoly. Even after funds for the enterprises at the Fort were disallowed, the structure became their place of refuge. The Christanna Indians' strategy of alliance and compliance with the English proved to be their salvation in a time when the riptides of intertribal and English violence tore apart many of the lesser tribes.

Over time Southeastern Indian tribes improvised many strategies to endure. Not all of those tribes were successful. The account of the Indian experiences at Fort Christanna is important for what it adds to this larger story. In Christanna's history we find an example of diminished tribes that, like many other Indian groups, bound themselves together and ensured their survival by forging critical new alliances. The Indian strategy at Fort Christanna was a unique one, however. The Saponie Tribes at Christanna moved to cultivate a favored status with the English in Virginia by complying fully with the will of the Governor and his Council. The Saponie Tribes solved their military and trade deficiencies with a political solution. As ambiguous as maintaining the English alliance was from a cultural perspective, it was a strategy that kept the people of the tribes alive and in community. In developing and sustaining the alliance, the Christanna Indians were not simply pawns being manipulated in an English game. The history of Fort Christanna tells us how in a dangerous time the Saponie Tribes took advantage of a unique relationship with the English to endure and forge their own futures.

Appendix I

The Signatures on the Treaty of Middle Plantation, 1677

The Thomas Jefferson Papers Series 8. Virginia Records Manuscripts. 1606-1737. Virginia Company of London and the Colony, 1606-92, Miscellaneous Papers

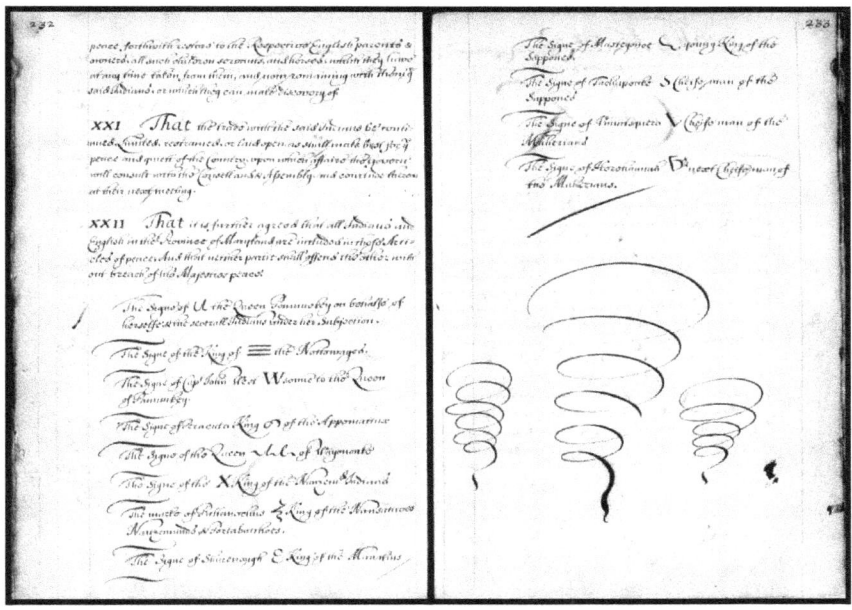

Appendix II

Signatures on the 1713/14 Treaty
The National Archives, London

Appendix III

Brunswick Patents & Deeds Marking the Boundaries of the Saponie Land (est. 1714)

West Line (called the "Upper Line") - South to North

VPB 34:279	12/May/1759	Benjamin Seawell	932a
VPB 13:393	28/Sept/1728	John Hix, Surry County	960a
VPB 13:211	13/Oct/1727	Daniell Hix, Brunswick Co.	355a
VPB 13:59	31/Oct/1726	George Hix Junr., Surry Co.	429a
VPB 12:51	7/Jul/1726	Daniel Hix of Surry County	137a
VPB 14:507	28/Sep/1732	Thomas Cock of Surry, Co.	1245a
BRDB 1:469-70	20-21/ Mar/1738/39	Thomas Cocke of Southwark Parish, Surry County to Samuel House	330a
VPB 29:396	10/Apr/1751	John Hall	355a
VPB 23:811	15/Mar/1744/45	John Hall	1800a

North Line - West to East

VPB 13:179	13/Oct/1727	George Hagood, Surry Co.	345a
BRDB 1:95-97		William Hagood to John Hagood	340a
VPB 14:535	28/Sep/1732	Henry Harrison, Surry Co.	2907a
VPB 13:175	13/Oct/1727	Charles Lucas	770a
VPB 13:360	28/Sep/1728	Henry Lound Edloe of Charles City County	406a
VPB 14:84	28/Sep/1728	William Keley of Brunswick County	248a
VPB 28:62	12/Jan/1746/47	James Keley, son and heir of William Keley	248a
VPB 17:496	9/Feb/1737/38	George Clark	400a

East Line (called the "Lower Line") - North to South

VPB 12:111	23/Oct/1724	Nathaniel Harrison of Surry County	4245a
VPB 14:534	28/Sep/1732	Henry Harrison, Surry Co. County	1888a
VPB 13:453	28/Sep/1728	Simon Gale, Surry Co.	500a

South line - East to West

VPB 13:441	28/Sep/1728	John Wall Junr., Brunswick Co.	387a

Appendix IV

Location of the Saponie Land Tract,
as established in 1714

Defined by Adjacent and Subsequent Brunswick County
Patents and Deeds

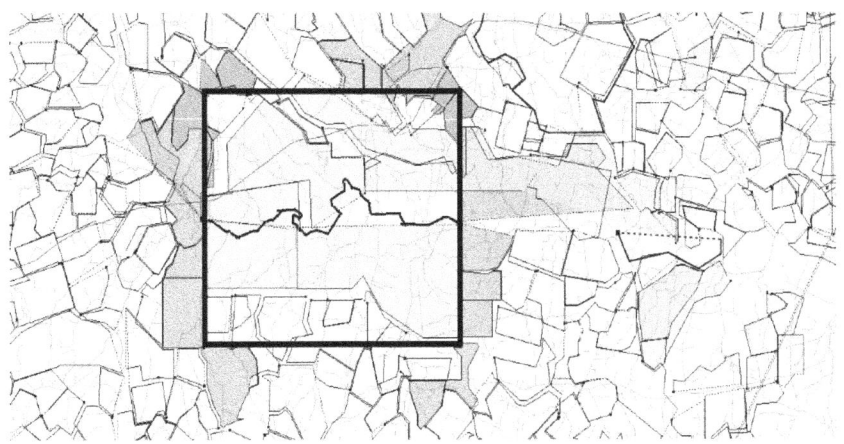

Darker gray tracts reference the "Indian Line" in the language of their patent or deed. These tracts frame the 36 square mile Saponie Land Tract.

The Meherrin River is shown meandering across the square of the tract.

Image generated using Deedmapper® software.

Appendix V

Portion of Gilmer Map 13, Depicting
Brunswick County, 1864
Road indicated by white arrows is likely a surviving
portion of the "Road to Junckatapurse"

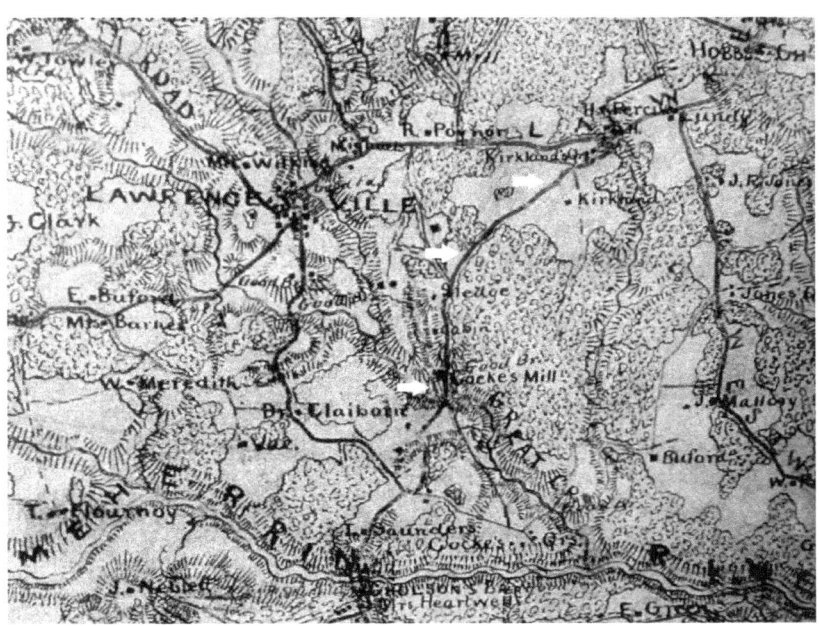

Map of Brunswick County Va. / made under the direction of Maj. A.H. Campbell P. Engr. C.S.A. in charge Topl Department D.N.Va. from surveys and reconnaissance by H.M. Graves Lt. P. Engrs . Nov 1864. Confederate States of America. Army. Dept. of Northern Virginia. Chief Engineer's Office; Graves, H. M, Surveyor.; Gilmer, Jeremy Francis, 1818-1883, USMA 1839 ; Campbell, Albert H. (Albert Henry), 1826-1899. Gilmer Map 13.

Appendix VI

Portion of the 1919 White Plains Topographical Map
Showing Jones Low Bridge

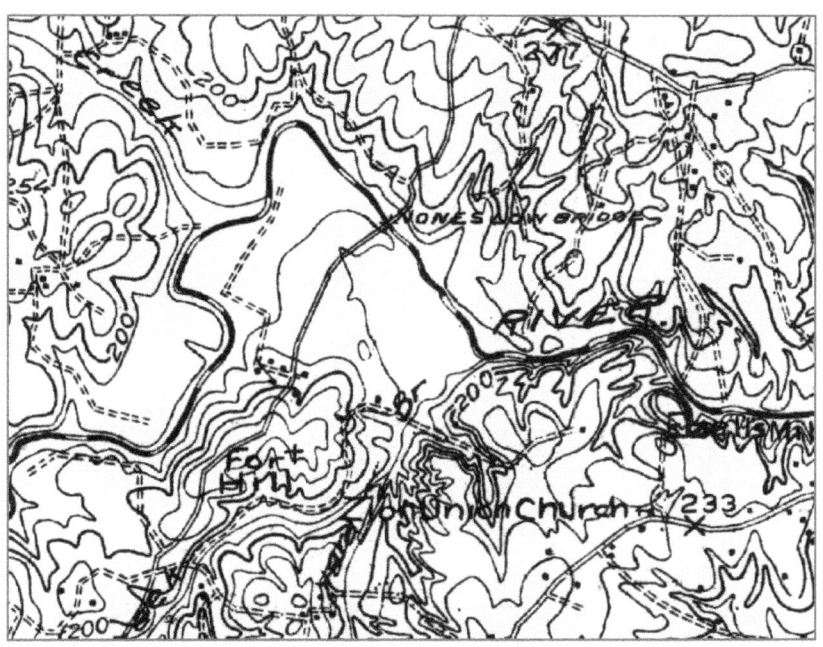

Appendix VII

"A Table of rates to barter by; viz., Quantity and Quality of Goods for Pounds of heavy drest Deer Skins"

A Gun	16
A Pound Powder	1
Four Pounds Bullets or Shot	1
A Pound red Lead	2
Fifty Flints	1
Two Knives	1
One Pound Beads	
Twenty-four Pipes	1
A broad Hoe	3
A Hatchet	2
A Pound Vermillion	16
A Yard double striped, yard-wide Cloth	3
A double striped Cloth Coat, Tinsey laced	16
A Half Thicks or Plains Coats, gartering laced	14
A Ditto, not laced	12
A Yard Strouds	4
A Yard Plains or Half thicks	2
A laced Hat	3
A plain Hat	2
A white Duffield Blanket	8
A blew or red Ditto, two yards	7
A course Linnen Shirt	3
A Gallon Rum	4
A Pound Vermillion, [and] two Pounds red Lead, mixed	20
Brass Kettles, per pound	2½
A Yard course flowered Calicoe	4
Three Yards broad scarlet Caddice	1

Table of Trade Goods and Exchange Rate from McDowell, W.L. ed., Journals of the Commissioners of the Indian Trade, September 20-1710-August 29, 1718. Columbia: South Carolina Archives Department. 1955, 269.

Notes

Notes for Introduction, pages ix-xvi

[1] Leonidas Dodson, *Alexander Spotswood: Governor of Virginia, 1711-1732*. (Philadelphia: University of Pennsylvania Press, 1932); Walter Havighurst, *Alexander Spotswood: Portrait of a Governor*. (Williamsburg, VA: Colonial Williamsburg, 1967). W. Stitt Robinson, *The Southern Colonial Frontier, 1607-1763*. (Albuquerque: University of New Mexico Press, 1979), 129-34. A noteworthy exception is Stephanie Gamble, "A Community of Convenience," *Native South* 6 (2013):70-109. Gamble's article focuses on the Saponi at Fort Christanna with an emphasis on tribal migrations.

[2] Mary C. Beaudry, "Colonizing the Virginia Frontier: Fort Christanna and Governor Spotswood's Indian Policy," chap. 7 in *Comparative Studies in the Archaeology of Colonialism*, ed. Stephen L. Dyson (Oxford: BAR, 1985).; Mary C. Beaudry, *Excavations at Fort Christanna, Brunswick County, Virginia, 1979 Season*, (Unpublished report, December 31, 1979); Mary Beaudry, "Fort Christanna and the Frontier and Early Fur Trade Artifact patterns: a Test," in Stanley South, "The Conference on Historic Site Archaeology Papers 1979 - Volume 14" (1982). Conference on Historic Site Archaeology Papers. Book 14, 46-58; Christopher

Stevenson, *Archaeological Excavations at Ft. Christanna 2001, Brunswick County Virginia.* (Unpublished report. Virginia Department of Historic Resources. Petersburg, VA, 24 September 2001); Christopher M. Stevenson et al, "Investigations into the European Provenance of Historic Gunflints from Fort Christanna, Virginia, through Trace Element Chemistry," *Archaeology of Eastern North America* 35 (2007): 49-62.

[3] See James H. Merrell, "Some Thoughts on Colonial Historians and American Indians," *William and Mary Quarterly*, 3rd ser. 46 no.1 (January 1989): 94-119 and his subsequent article "Second Thoughts on Colonial Historians and American Indians," *William and Mary Quarterly* 69 no.3 (July 2012):451-512.

[4] Daniel K. Richter, "War and Culture: the Iroquois Experience," *William and Mary Quarterly* 3rd ser. 40, no. 4 (October 1983): 528-59. See also William A. Starna and Ralph Watkins, "Northern Iroquoian Slavery," *Ethnohistory* 38, no. 1 (Winter 1991): 37-38, 52; William A. Fox looks at Iroquoian attacks from a demographic perspective, with an emphasis on the impact of diseases and disproportionate numbers of aggressive young male warriors in "Events as Seen from the North: Iroquois and Colonial Slavery," chap. 2 in *Mapping the Mississippian Shatter Zone*, ed. Robbie Ethridge and Sheri M. Shuck-Hall (Lincoln: University of Nebraska Press, 2009): 63-80.

[5] See Robbie Ethridge, "Creating the Shatter Zone: The Indian Slave Traders and the Collapse of the Southeastern Chiefdoms," chap. 10 in *Light on the Path: the Anthropology and History of the Southeastern Indians*, eds. Thomas J. Pluckhahn and Robbie Ethridge

(Tuscaloosa: University of Alabama Press, 2006): 207-18; Robbie Ethridge and Sheri M. Shuck-Hall, eds., *Mapping the Mississippian Shatter Zone* (Lincoln: University of Nebraska Press, 2009).

[6] Recent scholarship points to the Occoneechee as a primary early slaving society in the Southeast in the middle of the seventeenth-century. From an island location on the Roanoke River, the Occoneechee controlled the main trading path that connected the tribes of the Carolinas with the English trade goods flowing southwest out of Virginia. Though a relatively small tribe in comparison with larger Native groups to the south, the Occoneechee used their unique access to English goods and weapons, and their advantageous geographical situation to maintain for a time a dominant position among their Indian competitors, monopolizing the trade through intimidation and violence. Robin Beck attributes the failure of the Joara and the Wateree chiefdoms and their disappearance from the historical record to the activities of the Occoneechee as prime agents and controllers of the early militaristic slave trade in the Carolina and Virginia Piedmont. See Robin Beck, *Chiefdoms, Collapse, and Coalescence in the Early American South* (New York: Cambridge University Press, 2013), 135-36, 150-51. Occoneechee primacy in trade and regional warfare came to an abrupt end in 1676 when Nathaniel Bacon attacked the Occoneechee after the tribe had assisted Bacon's uncommissioned and illegal Virginia militia that defeated a body of Susquehannock Indians. Bacon's merciless attack on the Occoneechee severely reduced their population. From Bacon's account of the attack, we know that he and his rebel militia burned the Occoneechee king's forts and

"destroyed about 100 men and 2 of their kings, besides women and children." "Bacon's Rebellion," *William and Mary Quarterly* 9, no. 1 (July 1900): 7. Without the military strength to defend their island stronghold, to resist the relentless attacks by the Iroquois, and to perpetuate their regional control of Indian-English trade, the Occoneechee were forced to relocate to the south. In 1701, explorer and surveyor John Lawson found them in their town on the Eno River near present-day Hillsborough, NC. At that time the population of the once-feared tribe had dwindled to an estimated 75 individuals. See R. P. Stephen Davis, Jr. and H. Trawick Ward, "The Evolution of Siouan Communities in Piedmont North Carolina." *Southeastern Archaeology* 10, no. 1 (Summer 1991): 45-46. The Occoneechee in the quarter-century before Bacon's attack were very different from the remnant band that Lawson encountered, and that subsequently were joined with the Saponie and Tottero at Christanna.

Notes for Chapter One, pages 1-14

[1] For documentation of the details of this event, see Alexander Spotswood, *Official Letters of Alexander Spotswood,* vol. 2 (Richmond, VA: Historical Society, 1882-85), 147, 251, 257-59, 286-87; Henry Reed McIlwaine, ed., *Executive Journals of the Council of Colonial Virginia* (Richmond, VA: Virginia State Library, 1928), 3:442-43, 446; on the Catawba (Cattawbaw), see James R. Merrell, *Indian's New World: Catawbas and Their Neighbors from European Contact through the Era of Removal* (Chapel Hill: University of North Carolina Press, 1989), 76-79.

² McIlwaine, *Executive Journals,* 3:443, 450; Hugh Jones, *The Present State of Virginia* (New York, 1865), 12; Lawrence H. Leder, ed., *The Livingston Indian Records, 1666-1723.* (Gettysburg, PA: The Pennsylvania Historical Association, 1956), 222-23.

³ Spotswood, *Letters,* 2:225, 237; Merrell, *Indian's New World,* 78-79; Leder, *Livingston Indian Records,* 222-23.

⁴ Jones, *Present State of Virginia,* 15.

⁵ Ibid., 12; Leder, *Livingston Indian Records,* 222-23. Though it seems that Jones' identification of the man might have been a loose treatment of the facts for narrative purposes, *Wickmannatauchee,* in fact, did survive to appear before the Virginia Council two years later. McIlwaine, *Executive Journals,* 3:506.

⁶ McIlwaine, *Executive Journals,* 3:446.

⁷ An earlier letter to Hunter is preserved in William P. Palmer, ed., Calendar of Virginia State Papers and Other Manuscripts Preserved at the State Capitol at Richmond 1652-1781 (Richmond, VA: 1875), 179.

⁸ Spotswood made particular reference to this treaty. See Spotswood, *Letters,* 2:252; McIlwaine, *Executive Journals,* 3:450-51.

⁹ Davis, 40.

¹⁰ E. B. O'Callaghan, *Documents Relative to the Colonial History of the State of New York* (Albany, NY: 1855), 5:490-93.

¹¹ Carl Benn, "We Wish Not to Be Sold, the Iroquois Way of War," chap. 3 in *Iroquois in the War of 1812* (Toronto: University of Toronto Press, 1998). In particular, see page 78.

[12] William Byrd, *William Byrd's Histories of the Dividing Line Betwixt Virginia and North Carolina* (Raleigh, NC: Historical Association, 1929), 221.

[13] Jones, *Present State of Virginia*, 8.

[14] Charles Hudson, *The Southeastern Indians* (Knoxville: University of Tennessee Press, 1976), pp. 239-43.

[15] See Daniel K. Richter, "War and Culture," 528-59.

[16] Daniel K. Richter, *Trade, Land, Power* (Philadelphia: University of Pennsylvania Press, 2013), 71-3, 94-6. According to Richter, following the Tuscarora War, the 1713 move of the Lower Tuscarora northward to join with the Five Nations reinvigorated the mourning war practice in Iroquoia. The military attacks associated with this revitalized cultural pattern were directed primarily against the Catawba and the Southern tribes.

[17] Jones, Present State of Virginia, 17.

[18] Richter, *Trade, Land, Power*, 71.

[19] Ibid., 75-6.

[20] O'Callaghan, *Documents Relative to Colonial History*, 5:491.

[21] Edward Porter Alexander, ed., *The Journal of John Fontaine: An Irish Huguenot Son in Spain and Virginia 1710-1719* (Williamsburg, VA: The Colonial Williamsburg Foundation, 1972), 93.

[22] The tribal name was spelled variously "Jennitos," "Jennytoe," "Jenny Toe" and was used as a synonym for Seneca. See John Lawson, *A New Voyage to Carolina* (Chapel Hill: University of North Carolina Press, 1967), 53.

[23] O'Callaghan, *Documents Relative to Colonial History*, 5: 657-81; "Spotswood Concludes Peace with Iroquois at Albany," August 29, September 6, 12-12, 1722, in W. Stitt Robinson, Jr., ed., *Virginia Treaties, 1607-1722*, Vol. 4 of *Early American Indian Documents: Treaties and Laws, 1607-1789.* (Frederick, MD.: University Publications of America, 1983), 346-62; "Lancaster Treaty," June 22, 1744, in W. Stitt Robinson, Jr., ed., *Virginia Treaties, 1607-1722*, Vol. 5 of *Early American Indian Documents and Treaties, 1607-1789.* (Frederick, MD.: University Publications of America, 1983), 51-97.

[24] See Colin G. Calloway, *New Worlds for All: Europeans, and the Remaking of Early America* (Baltimore: Johns Hopkins University Press, 1997), 125-126; Yasuhide Kawashima, "The Role of Interpreters in Indian-White Relations on the Early American Frontier," *American Indian Quarterly* 13, no.1 (Winter, 1989), 1-14; Frederick Fausz, "Middlemen in Peace and War: Virginia's Earliest Indian Interpreters, 1608-1632," *The Virginia Magazine of History and Biography* 95, no.1. (January 1987), 42-43.

[25] McIlwaine, *Executive Journals*, 3:455; McIlwaine, *Executive Journals*, 4:178, 198.

[26] See Joseph M. Hall, *Zamumo's Gifts* (Philadelphia: University of Pennsylvania Press, 2009) 2, 5-11, 62-64; Tom Arne Midtrød, *The Memory of All Ancient Customs: Native American Diplomacy in the Colonial Hudson Valley* (Ithaca: Cornell University Press, 2012) 36-39; Wilbur R. Jacobs *Wilderness Politics and Indian Gifts* (Lincoln: University of Nebraska Press, 1966) 11, 13-19, 26.

[27] see Hudson, *Southeastern Indians*, 226-29, 317, 326-27, 336, 348, 373.

[28] Jones, 15.

[29] Lawson, J., *New Voyage to Carolina*, 63.

Notes for Chapter Two, pages 15-24

[1] Lawson, J., *New Voyage to Carolina*, xxxi- xxxvi.

[2] Spotswood, *Letters*, 145-46, 194.

[3] Cecil Headlam, ed., "America and West Indies: March 1714," *Calendar of State Papers Colonial, America and West Indies, Volume 27: 1712-1714*, [603, i-iii], British History Online, http://www.british-history.ac.uk/report.aspx?compid=73931

[4] Murray G. Lawson, "An Act for the Better Regulation of the Indian Trade, 1714," *Virginia Magazine of History and Biography*, 55, no. 4 (October, 1947): 329-32.

[5] "Treaty between Virginia and the Indians 1677," *Virginia Magazine of History and Biography*, 14, no.3 (January 1907): 289-96; "Treaty of Peace with Necotowance, King of the Indians," and "Treaty at Middle Plantation with Tributary Indians after Bacon's Rebellion" in Robinson, *Early American Indian Documents*, vol. 4: 67-70, 82-87.

[6] W. Stitt Robinson, Jr., "Tributary Indians in Colonial Virginia," *Virginia Magazine of History and Biography*, 67, no.1 (January, 1959): 60-63.

[7] Spotswood, *Letters*, 2:99, 197, 204.

[8] Ibid., 2:145.

[9] Ibid., 2:144.; Lawson, M. "Act for the Better Regulation," 330.

[10] Spotswood, *Letters*, 2:197.

[11] Ibid., 2:88, 113; McIlwaine, *Executive Journals*, 3:396-97; see also William Byrd, *Histories of the Dividing Line*, 308, 310. The use of "Saponie" in primary documents of the period does not typically refer to the "Saponie Tribe," but rather to the amalgamated group of tribes that lived in the town next to Fort Christanna. Spotswood initiated the use of the term in that way. We can speculate that Spotswood began doing this as a kind of shorthand for referring to all of the Siouan Indians living at Christanna, and that the Saponie Tribe was the strongest or most numerous of the tribes living at Christanna. There is a lack of consistency, however, in the 18th century use of the term "Saponie." At times the term "Saponie" does refer to the tribe itself or to a particular tribal individual, as we see in the Treaty of 1713/14. Even Spotswood used the term "Saponie" in 1720 and 1722 to refer to the single tribe. The writers of the period, however, were not concerned for the most part with a distinction between the Saponie tribe that settled with other tribes at Christanna, and the confederation of tribes that Spotswood called "Saponie." Thus the term "Saponie" was almost always synonymous with the term "Christanna Indians."

[12] Spotswood, *Letters*, 2:88; "Journal of the Lieut. Governor's Travels and Expenditures Undertaken for the Public Service of Virginia," *William and Mary Quarterly*, 2nd ser., 3, no.1 (January 1923): 42.

[13] McIlwaine, *Executive Journals*, 4:198.

Notes for Chapter Three, pages 25-44

[1] Spotswood, *Letters*, 2:302.

[2] Ibid., *Letters*, 2:88. In February and April of 1715 the Council gave the "Enoes" and groups living with them permission to join with the Saponie. They had not done so by April 1717. McIlwaine, Executive Journals, 3:396-97; "Journal of the Lieut. Governor's Travels," 44.

[3] An account of Christanna cannon is in "Brunswick County and Fort Christanna," *William and Mary Quarterly*, 9, no. 4 (April 1901): 214-18.

[4] Alexander, *Journal of John Fontaine*, 91.

[5] Stevenson, *Archaeological Excavations*.

[6] Mary Beaudry, Email message to author, 9 November, 2000; see Stevenson, *Archaeological Excavations*, feature 26.

[7] Headlam, "America and West Indies: July 1716," *Calendar of State Papers Colonial, America and West Indies, Volume 29: 1716-1717*, [243], *British History Online*, http://www.british-history.ac.uk/report.aspx?compid=74022&strquery=beresford

[8] David Hazzard and Martha McCartney, *Fort Christanna Archaeological Reconnaissance Survey*. (Unpublished report. Virginia Research Center for Archaeology, n.p., 1979; Stevenson, *Archaeological Excavations*, "Discussion," NP.

[9] Of the identifiable bones excavated at Ft. Christanna in the 1979 season, 86% was from swine and cattle. Mary C. Beaudry, *Excavations*, 54; David B. Landon, "Taphonomic Evidence for Site Formation Processes at

Fort Christanna," *International Journal of Osteoarchaeology* 2 (1992): 351-52.

[10] W. L. McDowell, ed., Journals of the Commissioners of the Indian Trade, Sept 20, 1710-August 29, 1718 (Columbia: S.C. Archives Department, 1955), 100-101.

[11] Headlam, "America and West Indies: July 1716"; Beaudry, *Excavations*, 62.

[12] McIlwaine, *Executive Journals*, 3:397.

[13] Alexander, *Journal of John Fontaine*, 91.

[14] Spotswood, *Letters*, 2:7.

[15] Ray R. Sasser and Dennis Hudgins, "Colonial Land Patents and the Search for Saponi Old Fort and Unote," *Archaeological Society of Virginia Quarterly Bulletin*, 50 no.2 (June 1995):19-25.

[16] Beaudry, *Excavations*, "Appendix"; Landon, 352.

[17] Regarding the date the Saponies and other tribes signed the 1677 Treaty, see Christian L. Feest, "Notes on Saponi Settlements in Virginia Prior to 1714," *Archaeological Society of Virginia Quarterly Bulletin* 28, no.3 (1974): 152.

[18] Spotswood, *Letters*, 2:88.

[19] McDowell, *Journal of the Commissioners*, 73, 236, 282, 307.

[20] Carol I. Mason, *Archaeology of Ocmulgee Old Fields, Macon, Georgia* (Tuscaloosa: Univ. of Alabama Press, 2005): 32.

[21] Alexander, *Journal of John Fontaine*, 93.

[22] The *Fry-Jefferson Map of Virginia* (1751) shows the "Trading Path leading to the Catawbau and Cherokee

Indian Nations" crossing the Meherrin River to the west of the newly relocated Brunswick County courthouse. Fort Christanna was located on the south side of the river and also west of the courthouse. For a discussion of the importance of the nexus of Indian paths in Virginia, see April Lee Hatfield, *Atlantic Virginia: Intercolonial Relations in the Seventeenth Century* (Philadelphia: University of Pennsylvania Press, 2007), esp. chap. 1, "Indian and English Geographies."

[23] John Lederer, *Discoveries of John Lederer*, ed. William P. Cumming (Charlottesville: University of Virginia, 1958), 27.

[24] *Temporary Acts #21*, Trott, New Collections (Columbia, SC: South Carolina Department of Archives and History): 126. [S165004]; William Byrd II's 1728 list of trade goods is similar. "The Goods for the Indian Trade consist chiefly in Guns, Powder, Shot, Hatchets (which the Indians call Tomahawks,) Kettles, red & blue Planes, Duffelds, Stroudwater blankets, and some Cutlary Wares, Brass Rings, and other Trinkets." Byrd, *Histories of the Dividing Line*, 298.

[25] Alexander, *Journal of John Fontaine*, 98.

[26] Spotswood, *Letters*, 2:225.

[27] Lawson, J. *New Voyage to Virginia*, 49-50, 53.

[28] Ibid., 31.

[29] A recent overview of this topic is found in Michael P. Morris, *The Bringing of Wonder: Trade and the Indians of the Southeast, 1700-1783* (Westport, CT: Greenwood Press, 1999). Especially see chaps. 2 and 4 on women and trade; James H. Merrell, " 'Our Bond of Peace': Patterns of Intercultural Exchange in the Carolina

Piedmont, 1650-1750," chap. 7 in *Powhatan's Mantle*, ed. Peter H. Wood, Gregory A. Waselkov, and M. Thomas Hatley, (Lincoln: University of Nebraska Press, 1989), 198, 200-201.

[30] Lawson, J., *New Voyage to Virginia*, 31, 39-42, 50, 167-68, 190; Byrd, *Histories of the Dividing Line*, 115-16.

[31] Merrell, "Bond." 198, 200.

[32] Spotswood, *Letters*, 2: 99, 197, 204.

[33] Ibid., 2: 197.

[34] McIlwaine, *Executive Journals*, 3:481.

[35] Alexander, *Journal of John Fontaine*, 97-98.

[36] Ibid., 98; Hugh Jones gives this similar description: "In their Rejoicings and Wardances they with the most antick Gestures, in the most frightful Dress, with a hideous Noise, enumerate the Enemies, that they have murder'd, and such like Exploits." Jones, 8.

[37] Alexander, *Journal of John Fontaine*, 9.

[38] Hudson, *Southeastern Indians*, 240, 244, 257.

Notes for Chapter Four, pages 45-66

[1] Sasser and Hudgins, "Colonial Land Patents," 20; see also Feest, "Notes on Saponi Settlements," 152-55.

[2] McIlwaine, *Executive Journals*, 3:188, 567; James Mooney argued for a separate Saponie town that was settled sometime before 1711 near present-day Windsor, NC (Bertie County). His primary evidence for this "Sapona Town" came from family stories shared in two personal letters penned by Mooney's

contemporary, Dr. E.W. Pugh, a resident of Windsor. To support his speculation regarding the "Sapona Town" in Bertie, Co., Mooney clearly draws incorrect inferences from period Virginia documents regarding the Saponie's involvement in the Tuscarora War. Given the traditional enmity between the Siouan Saponie and the Iroquoian Tuscarora, it is almost unthinkable that just before 1711 the Saponie would have settled in traditionally Tuscarora territory. Even the lure of trade would not have led the Saponie to build a town in such close proximity to an enemy tribe that greatly outnumbered them. Also contradicting Mooney's speculation is an abundance of documentary evidence from the period that tells us that from 1708-1713 the Saponie were settled in Virginia at *Unotee*. See James Mooney, *Siouan Tribes of the East* (Washington, D.C.: Government Printing Office, 1894), 42-43.

[3] Ibid., 3:510.

[4] Spotswood, Letters, 2:88.

[5] Sasser and Hudgins, "Colonial Land Patents," 20-23.

[6] Alexander, *Journal of John Fontaine*, 96.

[7] Ibid.

[8] Robert Beverley, *History and Present State of Virginia* (Chapel Hill: University of North Carolina Press, 1947), 174.

[9] Ibid., 176.

[10] John Swanton, *Indians of the Southeastern United States*, Smithsonian Institution Bureau of American Ethnology, Bulletin 137 (Washington, DC: Government Printing Office, 1946, 1969), 201; Spotswood estimated a population of 300. McIlwaine, *Executive Journals* 3:397.

[11] Alexander, *Journal of John Fontaine*, 97.

[12] Jones, *Present State of Virginia*, 9; Lawson, J. *New Voyage to Carolina*, 48-55.

[13] H. Trawick Ward and R. P. Stephen Davis, Jr., "Occaneechi Town: A Summary of Archaeological Findings," (2003) http://www.ibiblio.org/dig/html/part5/tab0.html

[14] Christopher M. Stevenson, "Archaeological Testing at a Native American Settlement (44Br156), Brunswick County, Virginia," (Unpublished manuscript, Virginia Department of Historic Resources, Petersburg, VA), 4; Davis, L. Davis, Maxham, Salvanish, Rodning, LaMorro, "Search for Sapony Village, Fort Christanna, VA" (Chapel Hill, NC: unpublished manuscript map, UNC, 2/8/2000-3/15/00); Beaudry, "Colonizing the Virginia Frontier," Note 3, n.p., mentions survey efforts of the Virginia Research Center for Archaeology, Col. Howard MacCord, Leverette Gregory and crew, and Charles Hodges that were attempts to locate Chunkete Posse, the Saponie town.

[15] Alexander, *Journal of John Fontaine*, 91, 93, 96, 99.

[16] Lewis Lochee. *Elements of Field Fortification* (London: T. Cadell, 1783; reprint, Oldwick, NJ: King's Arms Press & Bindery, n.d.), 37, 70.

[17] *An Introduction to the art of fortification, containing draughts of all the common works used in military architecture, and of the machines and utensils necessary either in attacks or defences...* (London: Printed for and sold by John Brindley, bookseller to his Royal Highness the Prince of Wales, at the Feathers in New Bond Street, 1745), n.p.

[18] Abel Boyer, *The Draughts of the most remarkable fortified towns of Europe, in 44 copper plates ...* (London, Printed for I. Cleave and J. Hartley: 1701), 7; a modern source for this distance is *The Oxford Essential Dictionary of the U.S. Military* (2001) that defines "musket shot" as 300 yards.

[19] Alexander, *Journal of John Fontaine,* 94-95; Edward P. Alexander, "An Indian Vocabulary from Fort Christanna," *Virginia Magazine of History and Biography* 79 (July 1971): 309-10; on the Siouan attribution of the language in Fontaine's vocabulary list, see also Ives Goddard, "Note on Alexander 1971," *International Journal of American Linguistics,"* 220. Goddard judged the general language in Fontaine's vocabulary clearly to be Siouan, very close to Tutelo, though mixed with words of non-Siouan origin. He concluded that non-Siouan words were spoken at Christanna possibly because they were part of a regional trade language or because they may have entered the vocabulary when non-Siouan refugees joined the other Indians at *Chunkete Posse.*

[20] Nathaniel Mason Pawlett, *Brunswick County Road Orders 1732-1746* (Charlottesville, VA: Virginia Transportation Research Council, July 1988, revised May 2004). 8, 16, 25.
Http://www.virginiadot.org/vtrc/main/online_reports/pdf/89-r1.pdf The road orders referenced in Pawlett are from *The Brunswick Order Book 1.* The particular dates and original pages are: 6 April 1733, 24, 6 Nov. 1735, 113, and 2 February 1738/39, 222.

[21] William Lindsay Hopkins, *Bath Parish register (births, deaths & marriages), 1827-1897 of Dinwiddie County,*

Virginia and St. Andrews Parish vestry book, 1732-1797 of Brunswick County, Virginia. (Richmond, VA: W.L. Hopkins, 1989). The latest date the Indian town name was used in processioning records was 25 Feb. 1792.

[22] Ibid., 64.

[23] Map #1: United States. Dept. of Interior, Geological Survey, Virginia, North Carolina, White Plains Quadrangle, edition of 1920 reprinted 1944.; Map #2: edition of 1919; Map #3: United States. Dept. of Interior, Gelogical Survey, Powellton Quadrant, edition for 1963.

[24] Headlam, "America and West Indies: February 1720, 1-8," *Calendar of State Papers Colonial, America and West Indies, Volume 31: 1719-1720,* [535i] *British History Online,* http://www.british-history.ac.uk/report.aspx?compid=74085&strquery=Christanna

[25] Beaudry, "Colonizing the Virginia Frontier," Note 3, n.p.

[26] Stevenson, *Archaeological Testing,* 11.

[27] Fontaine's text was transcribed as *machneto dufas,* but there is no f-consonant in any recorded Tutelo-Saponi vocabulary. See Horatio Hale, "The Tutelo Tribe and Language," *Proceedings of the American Philosophical Society,* 21 (March 1883): 15. It seems likely it was a transcription error. In the eighteenth-century, a manuscript "s" resembled a manuscript "f". Alexander, *Journal of John Fontaine,* 95; Alexander, "Indian Vocabulary," 310-11.

[28] Ibid., 94-95.

[29] Jones, *Present State of Virginia*. 11.

[30] Lawson, J., *New Voyage to Carolina*, 174.

[31] Jones, *Present State of Virginia*, 10.

[32] Alexander, *Journal of John Fontaine*, 93-94.

[33] Jones, *Present State of Virginia*, 11.

[34] Aaron Deter-Wolf and Tanya M. Peres, "Flint, Bone, and Thorns: Using Ethnohistorical Data, Experimental Archaeology, and Microscopy to Examine Ancient Tattooing in Eastern North America," *Zurich Studies in Archaeology*, 9 (2013): 35-45; Aaron Deter-Wolf, "Needle in a Haystack: Examining the Archaeological Evidence for Prehistoric Tattooing," chap. 2 in *Drawing with Great Needles: Ancient Tattoo Traditions of North America*, eds. Aaron Deter-Wolf and Carol Diaz-Granados (Austin: University of Texas Press, 2013): 42-72.

[35] Antoinette B. Wallace, "Native American Tattooing in the Protohistoric Southeast," chap. 1 in *Drawing with Great Needles: Ancient Tattoo Traditions of North America*, eds. Aaron Deter-Wolf and Carol Diaz-Granados (Austin: University of Texas Press, 2013): 1-41.

[36] Jones, *Present State of Virginia*, 8.

[37] Wilbur R. Jacobs, "Wampum: the Protocol of Diplomacy," *The William and Mary Quarterly*, 3rd Ser. 6, no. 4 (October 1949): 597-98, 601, 604.

[38] Midtrød, 36-8.

[39] Byrd, *Histories of the Dividing Line*, 308.

[40] Jones, *Present State of Virginia*, 8; See McIlwaine,

Executive Journals 3:510. This record mentions Saponie boys with a scalp that was taken.

[41] James Axtell and William C. Sturtevant, "The Unkindest Cut, or Who Invented Scalping," *The William and Mary Quarterly*, 37, no.3 (July 1980): 461-62, 467.

[42] Edward A. Sapir, "A Tutelo Vocabulary," *American Anthropologist*, n.s., 15, no. 2 (April-June 1913): 295. Sapir's phonetic rendering for "horse" (*tsʻuŋgidę̨ʻ ᵉ*) is the equivalent of Fontaine's rendering (*chunkete*) in his Christanna vocabulary. See Alexander, *Journal of John Fontaine*, 94.

[43] Ibid., 99.

[44] Byrd, pp. 308, 311-12.

[45] Lawson, J., *New Voyage to Carolina*, 44, 54.

[46] Alexander, *Journal of John Fontaine*, 94.

[47] Ibid., pp. 94-95. A comparison with the vocabulary collected by John Lawson reveals their different priorities. Lawson, J. *New Voyage to Carolina*, 233-39.

[48] Alexander, *Journal of John Fontaine*, 97.

[49] Jones, *Present State of Virginia*, 9.

[50] McDowell, *Journals of the Commissioners*, 269.

[51] Jones, *Present State of Virginia*, 10.

[52] Hudson, *Southeastern Indians*, 129, 223, 243-44, 326, 331, 357, 380; Stanley Pargellis, "An Account of the Indians in Virginia," *The William and Mary Quarterly*, 3rd Ser. 16, no. 2 (April 1959): 231; Lawson, J., *New Voyage to Carolina*, 28.

[53] Swanton, *Indians of the Southeast*, 528.

[54] Lawson, J., *New Voyage to Carolina*, 157-58.

[55] Ibid., 175.

[56] Ibid., 42.

[57] Byrd, *Histories of the Dividing Line*, 159-60.

[58] Ibid, 164.

[59] The Field Book of Alexander Irvine, a Carolinian who was a surveyor with the Dividing Line party, gives variant spellings for the creek names, but the "-mony" suffix indicating "water" is still present. See Colonial and State Records of North Carolina, "Field book of Alexander Irvine during the survey of the North Carolina/Virginia boundary, Irvine, Alexander, March 05, 1728 - October 26, 1728,"2: 811-12. http://docsouth.unc.edu/csr/index.html/document/csr02-0324 accessed 12/28/2015

Notes for Chapter Five, pages 67-75

[1] Susan Myrak Kingsbury, ed. *Records of the Virginia Company*, (Washington, DC:
Government Printing Office, 1933), 3:102.

[2] See Lyon G. Tyler, "Education in Colonial Virginia, Part I," *The William and Mary Quarterly* 5, no. 4 (April 1897): 219-23.

[3] William Walter Hening. *The Statutes at Large Being a Collection of All the Laws of Virginia, from the First Session of the Legislature, in the Year 1619.* (New York: R. & W. & G. Bartow, 1823): II:193.

[4] "The Charter of the College of William and Mary in Virginia," (1693), 5; "The Transfer of the College of

William and Mary," (1729), 42 in *The Officers, Statutes, and Charter of the College of William and Mary* (Philadelphia: William Fry Printer, 1817).

[5] William Stevens Perry, ed., *Historical Collections Relating to the History of the American Colonial Church*, (Hartford, CT: Church Press Company, 1870), 1:344.

[6] Alan Gallay, *The Indian Slave Trade: the Rise of the English Empire in the American South, 1670-1717* (New Haven: Yale University Press, 2002), 290.

[7] Perry, *Historical Collections*, 1:123.

[8] Bruce T. McCully, "Governor Francis Nicholson, Patron "Par Excellence" of Religion and Learning in Colonial America," *The William and Mary Quarterly* 39, no. 2 (April 1982): 316-18.

[9] Spotswood, *Letters*, 1:122.

[10] Ibid. The tribute in hides was a continuation of terms set down in the Treaty of 1646.

[11] Ibid., 174.

[12] Hening, I:396, II:193.

[13] Byrd, *Histories of the Dividing Line*, 118.

[14] Karen Stuart, *So Good a Work: the Brafferton School, 1691-1777*, (master's thesis, The College of William and Mary, 1984), 85-86. The son of a "Tottero King" apparently was one of the students at the College, but we do not know his name. In 1728 he was mortally wounded by a Nottoway man named Hickory, who he had met earlier at the College. McIlwaine, *Executive Journals*, 4:186.

[15] A transcription of the full treaty is in Robinson, *Early American Indian Documents,* vol. 4:82-87.

[16] Spotswood, *Letters,* 2:237.

[17] Ibid., 2:141.

[18] Ibid., 198; McIlwaine, *Executive Journals,* 3:408.

[19] McIlwaine, *Executive Journals,* 3:396.

[20] Alexander, *Journal of John Fontaine,* 98.

Notes for Chapter Six, pages 76-91

[1] Perry, *Historical Collections,* 1:196.

[2] Byrd, *Histories of the Dividing Line,* 118.

[3] Spotswood, *Letters,* 2:175.

[4] Ibid., 2:138.

[5] Palmer, *Calendar of Virginia State Papers,* 179.

[6] Landon, 351-52.

[7] "William Gordon to John Chamberlain," May 13, 1709, in *Colonial and State Records,* 1:708-15, *Documenting the American South,* http://docsouth.unc.edu/csr/index.html/document/csr01-0378

[8] "James Adams to John Chamberlain," October 4, 1709, in *Colonial and State Records,* 1:719-21, *Documenting the American South,* http://docsouth.unc.edu/csr/index.html/document/csr01-0384; See Herbert R. Paschal, "Charles Griffin," in William Powell, ed., *Dictionary of North Carolina Biography,* (Chapel Hill: University of North Carolina Press, 1986), 2:370-71; Herbert R. Paschal, "Charles

Griffin: Schoolmaster to the Southern Frontier," chapter 1 in East Carolina College, Department of History, *Essays in Southern Biography* (Greenville, NC, 1965): 1-16.

[9] Byrd, *Histories of the Dividing Line,* 118.

[10] Jones, *Present State of Virginia,* 14-15.

[11] Alexander, *Journal of John Fontaine,* 91.

[12] Ibid., 94-95; Alexander, "Indian Vocabulary," 307-13.

[13] McIlwaine, *Executive Journals,* 3:541.

[14] Perry, *Historical Collections,*1:196.

[15] Spotswood, *Letters,* 2:90, 196.

[16] McIlwaine, *Executive Journals,* 3:507.

[17] Hudson, *Southeastern Indians,* 260.

[18] Spotswood, *Letters,* 2:114.

[19] The first part of the name for this god appears to be a cognate of the Tutelo word for "Sun," See Hale, "Tutelo Tribe,"17, 43.

[20] Jones, *Present State of* Virginia,16.

[21] Lawson, J., *New Voyage to Carolina,* 219.

[22] Byrd, *Histories of the Dividing Line,* 200.

[23] William Powers, *Oglala Religion* (Lincoln: University of Nebraska Press: 1982): 53, 93-95; Joseph Epes Brown, *The Sacred Pipe* (Norman: University of Oklahoma Press, 1989), 29 n.13. The Lakota regarded the Milky Way as the W*anagi tacanku* or "ghost road" along which the souls of the dead walk at the conclusion of the Spirit Keeping rite (W*anagi yuhapi*). The belief was that *Maya owichapaha* judged the souls of the departed where the

Milky Way splits into two branches. Also see Gertrude P. Kurath, "The Tutelo Fourth Night Spirit Release Singing," *Midwest Folklore*, 4, no. 2 (Summer, 1954): 97-98. Kurath observed the same religious idea in Tutelo songs in the mid-1950s.

[24] Byrd, *Histories of the Dividing Line*, 178.

[25] Hudson, *Southeastern Indians*, 317-20.

[26] Beverley, *History and Present State of Virginia*, 191.

[27] "Journal of the Lieut. Governor's Travels," 44.

[28] McIlwaine, *Executive Journals*, 3:447.

[29] The 1713/14 Treaties with the Tuscarora and Nottoway called for those tribes initially to send their hostages to the Saponie Town.

Notes for Chapter Seven, pages 92-98

[1] Before Spotswood, Francis Nicholson had advocated a similar policy, and there was at the time of Fort Christanna a centralized Indian trade in New York. See Dodson, *Alexander Spotswood*, 83.

[2] During the controversy, William Byrd II, who was in London at that time, eventually joined those who opposed the monopoly. See Dodson, *Alexander Spotswood*, 93-95.

[3] McIlwaine, *Executive Journals*, 3:455-56; Dodson, *Alexander Spotswood*, 88-93.

[4] McIlwaine, *Executive Journals*, 3:456.

[5] Ibid., 479.

[6] Ibid., 456.

7 Dodson, *Alexander Spotswood*, 98.

8 McIlwaine, *Executive Journals*, 4:1.

9 Ibid., 4:33.

10 Spotswood, *Letters*, 2: 302; McIlwaine, *Executive Journals*, 3:483.

11 Spotswood, *Letters*, 2:303.

12 Headlam, "Calendar of State Papers Colonial, America and West Indies, Volume 31: 1719-1720 (February 1720, 1-8)"; McIlwaine, *Executive Journals*, 3:520.

13 McIlwaine, *Executive Journals*, 3:51, 520.

14 Ibid., 3:510, 512-13.

15 Hudson, *Southeastern Indians*, 229-30.

16 McIlwaine, *Executive Journals*, 3:510-11.

17 Ibid., 3:519; Headlam, "Calendar of State Papers Colonial, America and West Indies, Volume 31: 1719-1720 (February 1720, 1-8)."

Notes for Chapter Eight, pages 99-109

1 McIlwaine, *Executive Journals*, 3:517, 520.

2 Ibid., 3:532.

3 Ibid., 3:531, 534.

4 Ibid., 3: 552.

5 Ibid., 3:533-34.

6 Ibid., 4:144-45.

7 Palmer, *Calendar of Virginia State Papers*, 1:215; McIlwaine, *Executive Journals*, 4:186.

[8] McIlwaine, *Executive Journals,* 4:185-86, 189.

[9] Virginia. General Assembly. House of Burgesses, *Journals of the House of Burgesses of Virginia, 1727-34, 1736-40.* Edited by H. R. McIlwaine, (Richmond: The Colonial Press. E.Waddey Co. 1910), 64.

[10] McIlwaine, *Executive Journals,* 4:198.

[11] Cecil Headlam, ed., "America and West Indies: June 1729, 21-30," *Calendar of State Papers Colonial, America and West Indies, Volume 36: 1728-1729,* [796]; Byrd, *Histories of the Dividing Line,* 310.

[12] McIlwaine, *Executive Journals,* 4:198.

[13] Spotswood, *Letters,* 2:145.

[14] Ibid., 2:227.

[15] McIlwaine, *Executive Journals,* 4:133.

[16] Byrd, *Histories of the Dividing Line,* 310.

[17] McIlwaine, *Executive Journals,* 4: xlvii-lviii.

[18] Ibid., 3:515.

[19] Ibid., 526.

[20] Ibid., 4:180.

[21] Ibid., 4: 209.

[22] Merrell, *Indians New World,* 116.

[23] McIlwaine, *Executive Journals,* 4:269.

[24] Beck, *Chiefdoms,* 228-30.

[25] "Journal of the Liet. Governor's Travels," 44.

[26] James H. Merrell, "The Indian's New World: the Catawba Experience," *The William and Mary Quarterly* 41, no. 4 (October 1984): 541 n. 12.

[27] As a further note on the 1732 alliance, it seems that only a portion of the Saraw may have incorporated with the Saponie, or that the merger was temporary, for we know that some Saraw (Charraw, Cheraw) were documented as being settled with the Catawba as late as 1768. Swanton, 109-10.

[28] Gamble, "Community," 94.

[29] Robert J. Cain, ed. *Records of the Executive Council, 1735-1754.* Colonial Records of North Carolina, 2nd ser. (Raleigh, NC: Department of Cultural Resources, 1988), 8:304.

[30] McIlwaine, *Executive Journals*, 4:303.

[31] C.G. Holland, "A Saponi Note," *Archeological Society of Virginia Quarterly Bulletin*, 37 no.1 (1982): 42.

[32] Beaudry, *Excavations*, 54.

[33] Christopher Stevenson, "Christanna Pipestem Diameters." Unpublished spreadsheet, 2004.

Notes for Chapter Nine, pages 110-118

[1] Numerous gun parts were excavated at Fort Christanna, including firing hammers, gunflints, gun sights, trigger guards, ramrod pieces, birdshot and lead ball shot, though there is no way to determine whether these were associated with the English or the Native population at the fort. Some gun parts have been identified as parts for trade guns that were typically destined for the tribes. See Beaudry, *Excavations*, 47-52 and Stevenson, "Investigations," 49-62, that concludes through trace element analysis that all 65 gunflints found through the 1979-81 and 2001-2004 excavations

at the fort were of European origin.

² Jones, *Present State of Virginia*, 9; Alexander, *Journal of John Fontaine*, 97.

³ Lawson, J., *New Voyage to Carolina*, 213-14; Jones, *Present State of Virginia*, 16.

⁴ Jones, *Present State of Virginia*, 19.

⁵ Byrd, *Histories of the Dividing Line*, 118.

⁶ McIlwaine, *Executive Journals*, 3:549. Fires from Saponie hunting in 1721 were confused with the approach of "Southern Indians."

⁷ Byrd, *Histories of the Dividing Line*, 284-86; Jones, *Present State of Virginia*, 10.

⁸ Lawson, J., *New Voyage to Carolina*, 215.

⁹ Virginia State Archives, Orange County Order Book, no. 2, microfilm reel 30: no frame number, 1740; Virginia State Archives, Orange County Order Book, no. 3, microfilm reel 31: no frame number, May 12, 1742; See "Historical Notes and Queries," *Virginia Magazine of History and Biography*, 3, no.2 (1895): 190-91. At this time Spotswood had retired to a large tract of land in Spotsylvania County on the Rapidan River and near his other fort called Germanna. Initially this fort was populated by German immigrants the Governor had settled there to do iron mining.

¹⁰ Virginia State Archives, Orange County Order Book, no. 3. microfilm reel 31, frame number 309, Jan 1743. The names of those arrested were Alexander Machartoon, John Bowling, Maniniassa, Capt. Tom, Isaac, Harry, Blind Tom, Foolish Jack, Charles Griffin, John Collins, and Little Jack.

[11] McIlwaine, *Executive Journals,* 3:366; Byrd, *Histories of the Dividing Line,* 308, 310.

[12] McIlwaine, *Executive Journals,* 3:531, 534.

[13] O'Callaghan, *Documents Relative to Colonial History,* 5: 657-81.

[14] McIlwaine, *Executive Journals,* 4:152-53.

[15] Spotswood, *Letters,* 2:88.

[16] Byrd, *Histories of the Dividing Line,* 310, 312.

[17] McIlwaine, *Executive Journals,* 4:185, 189. Note that in their early contact with the tribes at Christanna, the Iroquois referred to all of the "Southern Indians" – Catawba and Christanns Indians – as *Toderechrones.* Five Nations documents have at least 14 variant spellings of that term. The name *Tutelo* was later used by the Five Nations tribes to refer more specifically to the *Tottero* people.

[18] O'Callaghan, *Documents Relative to Colonial History,* 6: 811-12.

[19] Hale, "Tutelo Tribe," 10.

[20] Mooney, 51.

[21] Raymond J. Demalie, "Tutelo and Neighboring Groups," in vol. 14 *of Handbook of North American Indians,* ed. Raymond D. Fogelson (Washington, D.C.: Smithsonian Institution, 2004), 296-97.

[22] McIlwaine, *Executive Journals,* 2:88.

[23] See Hale, "Tutelo Tribe," 36-45; Leo J. Frachtenberg, "Contributions to a Tutelo Vocabulary," American Anthropologist, n.s., 15, no. 3 (July-September 1913): 477-79; Sapir, 295-97; Gertrude P. Kurath, "The Tutelo

Fourth Night Spirit Release Singing," *Midwest Folklore*, 4, no. 2 (Summer, 1954): 87, 100.

[24] Demalie, "Tutelo," 297-298; for a list of documented Tutelo ceremonies see Jay Hansford C. Vest, "An Odyssey among the Iroquois: a History of Tutelo Relations in New York," *American Indian Quarterly* 29, no. 1/2 (Winter/Spring 2005): 126, n14; Gary Farmer (Cayuga), Email to author, February 11, 2018: "Yes. We still sing tutelo's songs and have tutelos relatives still living on the rez."

[25] McIlwaine, *Executive Journals*, 4:174.

[26] Byrd, *Histories of the Dividing Line*, 159.

[27] Forest Hazel, "Occaneechi-Saponi Descendants in the North Carolina Piedmont: The Texas Community," *Southern Indian Studies*, 40 (October 1991):7-8.

[28] William L. Saunders, ed. *Colonial Records of North Carolina* (Raleigh, NC: Josephus Daniels, 1887) 5: 162, 321.

[29] Benjamin J. Hillman, ed., *Executive Journals of the Council of Colonial Virginia* (Richmond, VA: Virginia State Library, 1966), 6:38.

[30] George Reese, ed., *Official Papers of Francis Fauquier* (Charlottesville: University Press of Virginia, 1981), 2:1017.

[31] "Observations of Superintendent John Stuart and Gov. James Grant of East Florida on the Proposed Plan of 1764 regarding the Future of Indian Affairs," *American Historical Review* 20, no.4 (July 1915): 825. In the same year the Board of Trade had sent to Governor Fauquier and others a proposed plan for future dealings with Indians. Included in that plan was a list of tribes, divided

into "Northern" and "Southern" Indians. The Saponie and Tottero were listed among the "Northern Indians," along with the Five Nations (then the Six Nations) and Pennsylvania tribes, supporting the evidence of a northern migration of Tottero ("Tuteeves") and Saponie ("Saponeys"). In 1768 the notable cartographer and surveyor, Thomas Hutchins, counted 30 "Sapòonies" with other tribes at Diahago (Tioga) far up the North (East) branch of the Susquehanna River, near the Pennsylvania border with New York. Thomas Jefferson, *Notes on the State of Virginia* (New York, Penguin Books, 1999), 110. John Stuart's observation, however, clearly indicates that a portion of the Saponie remained in Virginia. Reese, 1117.

[32] James Adair, *History of the American Indians* (London: Edward and Charles Dilly, 1775): 64.

[33] Ruth Y. Wetmore, "The Role of the Indian in North Carolina History," *North Carolina Historical Review,* 56 (April 1979), 170-72.

[34] Daniel Simpkins, *Aboriginal Intersite Settlement System Change in the Northeastern North Carolina Piedmont During the Contact Period* (Chapel Hill: University of North Carolina Press, 1992), 368.

[35] Bobbie Whitehead, "Tutelo Language Revitalized," *Indian Country Today* (June 7, 2005). http://indiancountrytodaymedianetwork.com/2005/06/08/tutelo-language-revitalized-96387 ; Gordon Debo Martin, "The 13th Annual Sappony Heritage Youth Camp 2014," *High Plains Echo* (July 2014), 5; "Occaneechi Language as Culture," *Occaneechi-Saponi Spring Pow Wow: Souvenir Commemorative Book* (June 7-8, 2002), n.p.; "*Mahk Jchi,*" performed by Ulali

(Hartford, CT: Original Vision Records, Corn Beans & Squash Music, 1994). Lyrics for the song, "Mahk Jchi," were translated into Tutelo-Saponi by Lawrence Dunmore (Occaneechi Band of the Saponi Nation).

Notes for Chapter Ten, pages 119-127

[1] For an overview of Native women's primary role in agriculture east of the Mississippi, see R. Douglas Hurt, *Indian Agriculture in America: Prehistory to the Present* (Lawrence: University Press of Kansas: 1987), 11-12, 31-32, 35-37, 40.

[2] Byrd, *Histories of the Dividing Line,* 286.

[3] Theda Perdue, *Cherokee Women: Gender and Culture Change, 1700-1835* (Lincoln: University of Nebraska Press, 1998), 64, 72, 76.

[4] Ibid., 309; Jones, Present State of Virginia, 9.

[5] Perry, Historical Collections, 1:196.

[6] Robinson, *Virginia Treaties,* vol. 4:243-44.

[7] Spotswood, *Letters,* 2:138.

[8] Lawson, J., New Voyage to Carolina, 51.

[9] McIlwaine, *Executive Journals,* 3:466, 474.

[10] See Gallay, *Indian Slave Trade.*

[11] See Daniel K. Richter. "War and Culture," 528-59.

[12] Gallay, *Indian Slave Trade,* 311.

[13] See for example Douglas H. Ubelaker,"Population Size, Contact to Nadir," in vol. 3 of *Handbook of North American Indian,* ed. Douglas H. Ubelaker (Washington, D.C.: Smithsonian Institution, 2006), 696, 699; Russell

Thornton, *American Indian Holocaust and Survival : A Population History Since 1492* (Norman: University of Oklahoma Press, 1987), xvii, 42-43.

[14] Virginia. General Assembly. House of Burgesses, *Journals of the House of Burgesses of Virginia, 1712-1714, 1715, 1718, 1720-1722, 1723-1726.* Edited by H. R. McIlwaine, (Richmond: The Colonial Press. E.Waddey Co., 1912), 197; See also McIlwaine, *Executive Journals*, 3:450.

[15] Samuel Hazard, ed., *Minutes of the Provincial Council of Pennsylvania* (Philadelphia: Jo. Severns & Company, 1862), 3:85, https://archive.org/stream/minutesprovinci05coungoog#page/n5/mode/1up

Notes for Overview, pages 128-134

[1] Merrell, "Bond," 196, 198, 200-02.

[2] Charles Hudson and others have used Imanuel Wallerstein's term, "modern world-system," to describe the global economic net that came with colonization and entangled all Southeastern Indians in the seventeenth- and eighteenth centuries. In Hudson's analysis, Southeastern tribes in the 1700s could survive the destructive effects of this world-system by staying in the Interior away from English interests or by providing to the English a valuable commodity they needed. Charles Hudson, "Why the Southeastern Indians Slaughtered Deer" in *Indians, Animals, and the Fur Trade*, ed. Shepard Krech III, (Athens, Georgia: University of Georgia Press, 1981), 166-70. More significantly for the Christanna Indians, however,

though they did both of these things to a certain degree, the Saponie Tribes maximized their chances of survival by allying themselves fully with the English, using the benefits of their Tributary status to gain protection and trade benefits.

[3] Beaudry, *Excavations*, 48-52, 62.

[4] Heather A. Lapham, *Hunting for Hides* (Tuscaloosa: University of Alabama Press, 2005) 138-9; Swanton, 445.

[5] Christopher Stevenson, Email to author, April 4, 2005.

Works Cited

Adair, James. *History of the American Indians.* London: Edward and Charles Dilly, 1775.

Alexander, Edward P. "An Indian Vocabulary from Fort Christanna, 1716." *Virginia Magazine of History and Biography* 70, no.3 (July 1971): 303-13.

Alexander, Edward Porter, ed. *The Journal of John Fontaine: An Irish Huguenot Son in Spain and Virginia 1710-1719.* Williamsburg, VA: The Colonial Williamsburg Foundation, 1972.

Axtell, James and William C. Sturtevant. "The Unkindest Cut, or Who Invented Scalping." *William and Mary Quarterly* 37, no.3 (July 1980): 451-472."Bacon's Rebellion." *William and Mary Quarterly* 9, no. 1 (July 1900): 1-10.

Beaudry, Mary C. "Colonizing the Virginia Frontier: Fort Christanna and Governor Spotswood's Indian Policy." Chap. 7 in *Comparative Studies in the Archaeology of Colonialism*, Edited by Stephen L Dyson. Oxford: B. A. R, 1985.

———. Email to author. November 9, 2000.

———. Excavations at Fort Christanna, Brunswick County, Virginia, 1979 Season. Unpublished report. December 31, 1979.

———. "Fort Christanna and the Frontier and Early Fur Trade Artifact Patterns: a Test" in Stanley South, "The Conference on Historic Site Archaeology Papers 1979 - Volume 14" (1982). *Conference on Historic Site Archaeology Papers. Book 14*, 46-58.

———. "Fort Christanna: Frontier Trading Post of the Virginia Indian Company." in *Forgotten Places and Things: Archaeological Perspectives on American History*. Edited by Albert E. Ward. Albuquerqe, N.M.: Center for Anthropological Studies. 1983. 133-40.

Beck, Robin. Chiefdoms, Collapse, and Coalescence in the Early American South. New York: Cambridge University Press, 2013.

Benn, Carl. *The Iroquois in the War of 1812*. Toronto: University of Toronto Press, 1998.

Beverley, Robert. *The History and Present State of Virginia*. Chapel Hill: University of North Carolina Press, 1947.

Boyer, Abel. The Draughts of the Most Remarkable Fortified Towns of Europe, in 44 Cooper Plates ... . London: Printed for I. Cleave and J. Hartley, 1701.

Brown, Joseph Epes. *The Sacred Pipe*. Norman: University of Oklahoma Press, 1989.

"Brunswick County and Fort Christanna." *William and Mary Quarterly* 9, no. 4 (April 1901): 214-18.

Byrd, William. William Byrd's Histories of the Dividing Line Betwixt Virginia and North Carolina. Raleigh, NC: Historical Association, 1929.

Cain, Robert J., ed. *Records of the Executive Council, 1735-1754*. Colonial Records of North Carolina, 2nd ser., vol. 8. Raleigh, NC: Department of Cultural Resources, 1988,

"The Charter of the College of William and Mary in Virginia," (1693) In *The Officers, Statutes, and Charter of the College of William and Mary.* Philadelphia: William Fry Printer, 1817, 5-25.

Calloway, Colin G. *New Worlds for All: Europeans, and the Remaking of Early America.* Baltimore: Johns Hopkins University Press, 1997.

Colonial and State Records of North Carolina, "Field book of Alexander Irvine during the survey of the North Carolina/Virginia boundary, Irvine, Alexander, March 05, 1728 - October 26, 1728," 2: 799-815. http://docsouth.unc.edu/csr/index.html/document/csr02-0324 accessed 12/28/2015

Cumming, William P. *Discoveries of John Lederer.* Charlottesville: University of Virginia, 1958.

Davis, Maxham, Salvanish, Rodning, LaMorro, L. Davis. "Search for Sapony Village, Fort Christanna, VA." Unpublished manuscript map. University of North Carolina, Chapel Hill, NC, February 8, 2000 - March 15, 2000.

Davis, R. P. Stephen, Jr. and H. Trawick Ward. "The Evolution of Siouan Communities in Piedmont North Carolina." *Southeastern Archaeology* 10, no. 1 (Summer 1991), 40-53.

Demallie, Raymond J. "Tutelo and Neighboring Groups," Vol. 14 of *Handbook of North American Indians,* Edited by Raymond D. Fogelson. Washington, DC: Smithsonian Institution, 2004, 286-300.

Deter-Wolf, Aaron. "Needle in a Haystack: Examining the Archaeological Evidence for Prehistoric Tattooing," chap. 2 in *Drawing with Great Needles: Ancient Tattoo Traditions of North America*, eds. Aaron Deter-Wolf and Carol Diaz-Granados (Austin: University of Texas Press, 2013): 42-72.

Deter-Wolf, Aaron and Tanya M. Peres. "Flint, Bone, and Thorns: Using Ethnohistorical Data, Experimental Archaeology, and Microscopy to Examine Ancient Tattooing in Eastern North America." Zurich Studies in Archaeology 9 (2013): 35-45.

Dodson, Leonidas. *Alexander Spotswood: Governor of Virginia, 1711-1732*. Philadelphia: University of Pennsylvania Press, 1932.

Ethridge, Robbie. "Creating the Shatter Zone: the Indian Slave Traders and the Collapse of the Southeastern Chiefdoms." chap. 10 in *Light on the Path: the Anthropology and History of the Southeastern Indians*. Edited by Thomas J. Pluckhahn and Robbie Ethridge. Tuscaloosa: University of Alabama Press, 2006, 207-18.

Ethridge, Robbie and Sherri M. Shuck-Hall, eds. *Mapping the Mississippian Shatter Zone*. Lincoln: University of Nebraska Press, 2009.

Fausz, Frederick. "Middlemen in Peace and War: Virginia's Earliest Indian Interpreters, 1608-1632." *Virginia Magazine of History and Biography* 95, no. 1 (January 1987): 41-64.

Feest, Christian L. "Notes on Saponi Settlements in Virginia Prior to 1714." *Archeological Society of Virginia Quarterly Bulletin* 28, no. 3 (1974):152.

Fox, William A. "Events as Seen from the North: Iroquois and Colonial Slavery." chap. 2 in *Mapping the Mississippian Shatter Zone*. Edited by Robbie Ethridge and Sherri M. Shuck-Hall. Lincoln: University of Nebraska Press, 2009, 63-80.

Frachtenberg, Leo J. "Contributions to a Tutelo Vocabulary." *American Anthropologist*, n.s., 15, no. 3 (July-September 1913): 477-79.

Gallay, Alan. The Indian Slave Trade: The Rise of the English Empire in the American South, 1670-1717. New Haven, CT: Yale University Press, 2002.

Gamble, Stephanie. "A Community of Convenience." *Native South* 6 (2013): 70-109.

Goddard, Ives. "Note on Alexander 1971," *International Journal of American Linguistics*," 220.

Hale, Horatio. "The Tutelo Tribe and Language." *Proceedings of the American Philosophical Society* 21(1883): 1-47.

Hall, Joseph M., *Zamumo's Gifts: Indian European Exchange in the Colonial Southeast* Philadelphia: University of Pennsylvania Press, 2009.

Hatfield, April Lee. *Atlantic Virginia: Intercolonial Relations in the Seventeenth Century*. Philadelphia: University of Pennsylvania Press, 2007.

Havighurst, Walter. *Alexander Spotswood: Portrait of a Governor*. Williamsburg, VA: Colonial Williamsburg, 1967.

Hazel, Forest. "Occaneechi-Saponi Descendants in the North Carolina Piedmont: The Texas Community." *Southern Indian Studies* 40 (October 1991): 3-30.

Hazard, Samuel, ed. *Minutes of the Provincial Council of Pennsylvania.* Vol. 3. Philadelphia: Jo. Severns & Company, 1862. http://archive.org/stream/minutesporvince05coungoo g#page/n5/mode/1up

Hazzard, David and Martha McCartney. *Fort Christanna Archaeological Reconnaissance Survey.* Unpublished report. Virginia Research Center for Archaeology, 1979.

Headlam, Cecil, ed. "American and West Indies, March 1714." *Calendar of State Papers Colonial, America and West Indies, Volume 27: 1712-1714. British History Online.* http://www.british-history.ac.uk/report.aspx?compid=73931

Headlam, Cecil, ed. "American and West Indies." *Calendar of State Papers Colonial, America and West Indies, Volume 29: 1716-1717. British History Online.* http://www.british-history.ac.uk/report.aspx?compid=74022&strquery=beresford

Headlam, Cecil, ed. "American and West Indies." *Calendar of State Papers Colonial, America and West Indies, Volume 31: 1719-1720. British History Online.* http://www.british-history.ac.uk/report.aspx?compid=74085&strquery=Christanna

William Walter Hening. The Statutes at Large Being a Collection of All the Laws of Virginia, from the First Session of the Legislature, in the Year 1619. New York: R. & W. & G. Bartow, 1823.

Hillman Benjamin J., ed. *Executive Journal of the Council of Colonial Virginia*. Vol. 6. Richmond, VA: Virginia State Library, 1966.

"Historical Notes and Queries." *Virginia Magazine of History and Biography*. 3, no. 2 (1895):189-207.

Holland, G.C. "A Saponi Note." *Archeological Society of Virginia Quarterly Bulletin*, 37 no.1 (1982): 42.

Hopkins, William Lindsay. Bath Parish register (births, deaths & marriages), 1827-1897 of Dinwiddie County, Virginia and St. Andrews Parish vestry book, 1732-1797 of Brunswick County, Virginia. Richmond, VA: W.L. Hopkins, 1989.

Hudson, Charles. *The Southeastern Indians*. Knoxville: University of Tennessee Press, 1976.

———. "Why the Southeastern Indians Slaughtered Deer." chap. 7 in *Indians, Animals, and the Fur Trade*. Edited by Shepard Krech III. Athens, Georgia: University of Georgia Press, 1981, 157-76.

Hurt, R. Douglas. *Indian Agriculture in America: Prehistory to the Present*. Lawrence: University Press of Kansas: 1987.

An Introduction to the art of fortification, containing draughts of all the common works used in military architecture, and of the machines and utensils necessary either in attacks or defenses... London: Printed for and sold by John Brindley, bookseller to his Royal Highness the Prince of Wales, at the Feathers in New Bond Street, 1745.

Jacobs, Wilbur R. "Wampum: The Protocol of Indian Diplomacy." *The William and Mary Quarterly*, 3rd ser. 6, no. 4 (October 1949): 596-604.

———. Wilderness politics and Indian Gifts: the Northern Colonial Frontier, 1748-1763. Lincoln: University of Nebraska Press, 1966.

"James Adams to John Chamberlain, October 4, 1709." in *Colonial and State Records*, 1: 719-21, *Documenting the American South*. http://docsouth.unc.edu/csr/index.html/document/csr01-0384.

Jefferson, Thomas. *Notes on the State of Virginia*. New York: Penguin Books, 1999.

Jones, Hugh. *Present State of Virginia*. New York, 1865.

"Journal of the Lieut. Governor's Travels and Expenditures Undertaken for the Public Service of Virginia." *William and Mary Quarterly 2nd ser.*, 3, no. 1 (January 1923): 40-45.

Kawashima, Yasuhide. "The Role of Interpreters in Indian-White Relations on the Early American Frontier." *American Indian Quarterly* 13, no. 1 (Winter 1989): 1-14.

Kingsbury, Susan Myrak, ed. Records of the Virginia Company. Vol. 1. Washington, DC: Government Printing Office, 1933.

Kurath, Gertrude P. "The Tutelo Fourth Night Spirit Release Singing," *Midwest Folklore*, 4, no. 2 (Summer, 1954): 87 - 105.

Landon, David B. "Taphonomic Evidence for Site Formation Processes at Fort Christanna," *International Journal of Osteoarchaeology* 2 (1992): 351-59.

Lapham, Heather A. *Hunting for Hides.* Tuscaloosa: University of Alabama Press, 2005.

Lawson, John. *A New Voyage to Carolina.* Chapel Hill: University of North Carolina Press, 1967.

Lawson, Murray G. "An Act for the Better Regulation of the Indian Trade, 1714." *Virginia Magazine of History and Biography* 55, no. 4 (October 1947): 329-32.

Leder, Lawrence H., ed. *The Livingston Indian Record, 1666-1723.* Gettysbury, PA: The Pennsylvania Historical Association, 1956.

Lederer, John. *Discoveries of John Lederer.* Edited by William P. Cumming. Charlottesville: University of Virginia Press, 1958.

Lochee, Lewis. *Elements of Field Fortification.* London: T. Cadell, 1783. Reprint, Old Wick, NJ: Kings Arms Press and Bindery, n.d.

McCully, Bruce T. "Governor Francis Nicholson, Patron "par Excellence" of Religion and Learning in Colonial America.". *The William and Mary Quarterly* 39.2 (1982): 310–333.

McDowell, W. L., ed. Journals of the Commissioners of the Indian Trade, Sept. 20, 1710-August 29, 1718. Columbia: S.C. Archives Department, 1955.

McIlwaine, Henry Reed, ed. *Executive Journals of the Council of Colonial Virginia.* Vols. 3 & 4. Richmond, VA: Virginia State Library, 1928, 1930.

"*Mahk Jchi*," performed by Ulali. Hartford, CT : Original Vision Records, Corn Beans & Squash Music,1994.

Map #1: United States. Dept. of Interior, Geological Survey, Virginia, North Carolina, White Plains Quadrangle, edition of 1920 reprinted 1944.; Map #2: edition of 1919; Map #3: United States. Dept. of Interior, Gelogical Survey, Powellton Quadrant, edition for 1963.

Martin, Gordon Debo. "The 13th Annual Sappony Heritage Youth Camp 2014," *High Plains Echo* (July 2014): 5.

Mason, Carol I. *Archaeology of Ocmulgee Old Fields, Macon, Georgia.* Tuscaloosa: University of Alabama Press, 2005.

Merrell, James H. "The Indian's New World: the Catawba Experience.gamble" *The William and Mary Quarterly* 41, no. 4 (October 1984): 537 - 565.

———. Indian's New World: Catawbas and Their Neighbors from European Contact through the Era of Removal. Chapel Hill: University of North Carolina Press, 1989.

———. "'Our Bond of Peace'" Patterns of Intercultural Exchange in the Carolina Piedmont, 1650-1750." chap. 7 in *Powhatan's Mantle*. Edited by Peter H. Wood, Gregory A. Waselkov, and M. Thomas Hatley. Lincoln: University of Nebraska Press, 1989, 196-222.

———. "Second Thoughts on Colonial Historians and American Indians." *William and Mary Quarterly* 69, no. 3 (July 2012): 451-512.

———. "Some Thoughts on Colonial Historians and American Indians." *William and Mary Quarterly* 46, no. 1 (January 1989): 94-119.

Midtrød, Tom Arne. The Memory of All Ancient Customs: Native American Diplomacy in the Colonial Hudson Valley. Ithaca: Cornell University Press, 2012.

Mooney, James. *Siouan Tribes of the East*. Washington, DC: Government Printing Office, 1894.

Morris, Michael P. The Bringing of Wonder: Trade and the Indians of the Southeast, 1700-1783. Westport, CT: Greenwood Press, 1999.

"Observations of Superintendent John Stuart and Gov. James Grant of East Florida on the Proposed Plan of 1764 regarding the Future of Indian Affairs." *American Historical Review* 20, no. 4 (July 1915):815-31.

O'Callaghan, E. B. *Documents Relative to the Colonial History of the State of New York*. Vols. 5 and 6. Albany, NY: Weed, Parsons, and Co., 1855.

"Occaneechi Language as Culture." Occaneechi-Saponi Spring Pow Wow: Souvenir Commemorative Book (June 7-8, 2002): n.p.

Palmer, William P., ed. Calendar of Virginia State Papers and Other Manuscripts Preserved at the State Capitol at Richmond, 1652-1781. Richmond, VA, 1875.

Pargellis, Stanley, "An Account of the Indians in Virginia," *The William and Mary Quarterly* 3rd ser. 16, no. 2 (April 1959): 228-43.

Paschal, Herbert R. "Charles Griffin: Schoolmaster to the Southern Frontier." chap. 1 in East Carolina College. Department of History. *Essays in Southern Biography*. Greenville, NC, 1965.

Paschal, Herbert R. "Griffin, Charles." In *Dictionary of North Carolina Biography*, Edited by William E. Powell.

Chapel Hill: University of North Carolina Press, 1986, 370-71.

Pawlett, Nathaniel Mason. *Brunswick County Road Orders 1732-1746*. Charlottesville, VA: Virginia Transportation Research Council, July 1988. Revised May 2004. http://www.virginiadot.org/vtrc/main/online_reports/pdf/89-r1.pdf

Perdue, Theda. *Cherokee Women: Gender and Culture Change, 1700-1835*. Lincoln: University of Nebraska Press, 1998.

Perry, William Stevens, ed. *Historical Collections Relating to the History of the American Colonial Church*, Vol. I. Hartford, CT: Church Press Company, 1870.

Powers, William. *Oglala Religion*. Lincoln: University of Nebraska Press: 1982.

Reese, George, ed. *Official Papers of Francis Fauquier*, Vol. 2. Charlottesville: University Press of Virginia, 1981.

Richter, Daniel K. *Trade, Land, Power*. Philadelphia: University of Pennsylvania Press, 2013.

———. "War and Culture: the Iroquois Experience," *William and Mary Quarterly* 40, no. 4 (October 1983): 528-59.

Robinson, W. Stitt, Jr. *The Southern Colonial Frontier, 1607-1763*. Albuquerque: University of New Mexico Press, 1979.

———. "Tributary Indians in Colonial Virginia." *Virginia Magazine of History and Biography*. 67, no. 1 (January 1959): 49-64.

Robinson, W. Stitt, Jr., ed. *Virginia Treaties, 1607-1722*. Vols. 4 & 5 of *Early American Indian Documents: Treaties and Laws, 1607-1789*. Frederick, MD.: University Publications of America, 1983.

Sapir, Edward A. "A Tutelo Vocabulary," *American Anthropologist*, n.s., 15, no. 2 (April – June 1913): 295-97.

Sasser, Ray R., and Dennis Hudgins. "Colonial Land Patents and the Search for Saponi Old Fort and Unote." *Archaeological Society of Virginia Quarterly Bulletin* 50, no. 2 (June 1995): 19-25.

Saunders, William L., ed. *Colonial Records of North Carolina*. Raleigh, NC: Josephus Daniels, 1887.

Simpkins, Daniel. Aboriginal Intersite Settlement System Change in the Northeastern North Carolina Piedmont during the Contact Period. Chapel Hill: University of North Carolina Press, 1992.

Spotswood, Alexander. *Official Letters of Alexander Spotswood*. 2 vols. Richmond, VA: Historical Society, 1885.

Starna, William A. and Ralph Watkins, "Northern Iroquoian Slavery," *Ethnohistory* 38, no.1 (Winter 1991): 34-57.

Stevenson, Christopher M. "Archaeological Excavations at Fort Christanna 2001, Brunswick County, Virginia." Unpublished report. Virginia Department of Historic Resources, Petersburg, VA, 24 September 2001.

———. "Archaeological Testing at a Native American Settlement (44Br156), Brunswick County, Virginia." Unpublished report. Virginia Department of Historic Resources, Petersburg, VA, n.d.

———. "Christanna Pipestem Diameters". Unpublished spreadsheet, 2004.

———. Email to author, April 4, 2005.

Stevenson, Christopher M., Emily Bikowski, Hector Neff, Michel Orliac, Colin Pendleton "Investigations into the European Provenance of Historic Gunflints from Fort Christanna, Virginia, through Trace Element Chemistry," *Archaeology of Eastern North America*. 35 (2007): 49-62.

Stuart, Karen Ann. *"So good a work": the Brafferton school, 1691-1777*. Thesis (M.A.)—College of William and Mary, 1984.

Swanton, John R. *Indians of the Southeastern United States*. Smithsonian Institution Bureau of American Ethnology Bulletin 137. Washington, DC: Government Printing Office, 1946. Reprint 1969.

Temporary Acts, #21, Trott, New Collections. Columbia, SC: South Carolina Department of Archives and History. [S165004]

Thornton, Russell. American Indian Holocaust and Survival : A Population History Since 1492. Norman: University of Oklahoma Press, 1987.

"The Transfer of the College of William and Mary," (1729) In *The Officers, Statutes, and Charter of the College of William and Mary* Philadelphia: William Fry Printer, 1817, 26-50.

"Treaty between Virginia and the Indians 1677." *Virginia Magazine of History and Biography* 14, no. 3 (January 1907): 289-96.

Tyler, Lyon G. "Education in Colonial Virginia, Part I," *The William and Mary Quarterly* 5, no. 4 (April 1897): 219-23.

Ubelaker, Douglas H. "Population Size, Contact to Nadir," Vol. 3 of *Handbook of North American Indian*, Edited by Douglas H. Ubelaker. Washington, DC: Smithsonian Institution, 2006), 694-701.

Vest, Jay Hansford C., "An Odyssey among the Iroquois: A History of Tutelo Relations in New York," *American Indian Quarterly* 29, no. 1-2 (Winter-Spring 2005), 124-55.

"Virginia Council Records." *Virginia Magazine of History and Biography* 33, no. 2 (April 1925): 175-93.

Virginia. General Assembly. House of Burgesses, *Journals of the House of Burgesses of Virginia, 1712-1714, 1715, 1718, 1720-1722, 1723-1726*. Edited by H. R. McIlwaine. Richmond, VA: The Colonial Press. E. Waddey Co., 1912.

Virginia. General Assembly. House of Burgesses, *Journals of the House of Burgesses of Virginia, 1727-34, 1736-40*. Edited by H. R. McIlwaine, Richmond: The Colonial Press. E. Waddey Co., 1910.

Virginia State Archives, Orange County, Order Book, no. 2. Microfilm reel 30: no frame number, 1740.

Virginia State Archives, Orange County, Order Book, no. 3. Microfilm reel 31: no frame number, May 12, 1742.

Wallace, Antoinette B. "Native American Tattooing in the Protohistoric Southeast." chap. 1 in *Drawing with Great Needles: Ancient Tattoo Traditions of North America*, eds. Aaron Deter-Wolf and Carol Diaz-

Granados (Austin: University of Texas Press, 2013): 1-41.

Ward, H. Trawick and R. P. Stephen Davis, Jr. "Occaneechi Town: a Summary of Archaeological Findings." (2003) http://www.ibiblio.org/dig/html/part5/tab0.html

Wetmore, Ruth Y. "The Role of the Indians in North Carolina History." *North Carolina Historical Review* 56 (April 1979): 162-76.

Whitehead, B. (2005, June 7). "Tutelo Language Revitalized." *Indian Country Today*. Retrieved from http://indiancountrytodaymedianetwork.com/2005/06/08/tutelo-language-revitalized-96387

"William Gordon to John Chamberlain, May 13, 1709." In *Colonial and State Records*, 1:708-715, *Documenting the American South.* http://docsouth.unc.edu/csr/index.html/document/csr01-0378

Wood, Peter H., et al, eds. *Powhatan's Mantle*. Lincoln: University of Nebraska Press, 1989.

Index

Act for the Better Regulation of the Indian Trade, viii, 17, 19, 34, 72, 93
Adshusheer, 13
archaeology and archaeological, iv, ix-xi, 26-28, 30-31, 49, 53, 56, 78-79, 109, 130
Articles of Peace (1677), 16-17, 21, *see also* Treaty of Middle Plantation

Bearskin (Bear-skin), Ned, 58, 65, 84-87, 110-111
Beaudry, Mary, iv, 53, 109
Beverley, Robert, 47, 61, 88
blankets, 16, 36, 48, 55, 60-62, 66, 98, 110, 131, 142
Blunt, Tom, 108
Brunswick County, iii, 22, 51-52, 81, 115
Byrd II, William, 5-6, 39, 58-59, 61, 65-66, 71, 77, 80, 85, 87, 103, 107, 111, 113, 115-116, 120

cannon, xvii, 26, 30, 37, 49, 96
Catawba, 1-9, 15-16, 34-35, 37-38, 73, 75, 88-89, 94, 101-102, 104-107, 113, 122, 124-127, 132
Cayuga, 4, 9, 33, 114-115
Cherokee, 16, 94, 100, 120
Chickasaw, 94, 100
Chiskiak, 23
Christanna, *passim*
Chunkete Posse (var. Chunketapusso) x, xv, 46, 50-53, 58-59, 76-77, 79, 89-91, 96, 102-103, 105, 107, 110, 113, 115, 118-122, 124, 129, *see also* Junckatapurse
cows, 121

disallowance, 92-95

firearms, 21, 30, 40-41, 62, 110, 122, 130, *see also* musket
Fort Christanna, *passim*

Genito, 9-10, 15, 33, 66, 75, 116
Gingaskin, 23
Gooch, William, viii, 102, 105, 108-109
Graffenried, Baron von, 16
Griffin, Charles, 2, 28, 50, 77, 79-82, 88, 90, 112, 120
gun, 27, 35-36, 62, 94, 117, 122, 130, 142
gunpowder, *see* powder

Hancock, Chief, 16
Haudenosaunee, 4, 114, *see also* Iroquois
Hix, Robert, 29-30, 40, 69, 95, 108
Hoonskey or Hoontky, vii, 9, 19, 33
Hoontkymiha, vii, 19, 33, 121

Indian School, 2, 15, 110-111, 126
Iroquois or Iroquoia, xiii, 4-8, 98, 105, 114-115, *see also Haudenosaunee*
Jones, Rev. Hugh, 3-4, 6-7, 12, 48, 54-58, 61, 65, 80, 84-85, 110-111
Junckatapurse (var. *Jackatapurse, Jounkatapouse, Juckatapurse, Junckataourse, Junkatapouse*), 51-52, 115, 140, *see also* Chunkete Posse

Keyauwee, 107, 121
kinship, 6, 56, 58, 107

labor, 27-41, 83
language, vii, xiv, 2, 8, 10, 19-20, 38, 50, 56, 59, 65, 70, 72, 75, 80, 84, 88-89, 107, 111, 113-116, 118, 129
Lawson, 13, 16, 37-39, 48-49, 55, 59-61, 63-64, 84, 88, 107, 110-111, 121

marriage, 7, 38, 106-107, 114
matrilineal, 121
Mattaponi, 23
meat 43, 79, 86-87

Meherrin (river), 1, 22, 25, 46, 49, 51-53, 139
Meherrin (tribe), 17, 23, 34, 36-37, 45, 70, 74-75, 96-97, 117
Mississippian Shatter Zone, xiv
Mohawk, 4-5, 7, 9, 37
Mohomny, 84-86
monopoly, 34, 92-93, 129, 133
musket, 2, 32, 49-50, 111, 122-123, 130, 133

Nicholson, Francis, viii, 69-70, 82
Northern Tribes, 4, 33, 41, 88, 122, 129, see also Iroquois
Nottoway, 17, 22, 34, 70, 74, 96-98, 101, 108, 113, 117
Occaneechi, ii, 116, 118
Occoneechee, vi, xii, xiii n.6, 2, 11, 17, 19, 22, 31, 33, 46, 49, 88, 107, 114, 121
Oneida, 4
Onondaga, 4, 5, 96, 98

Pamunkey, 23, 70, 117
pecoon or puckoone, 63-64

powder, 9, 16, 19, 21, 30, 35-36, 40-41, 56, 62-63, 66, 89, 94, 98, 101, 122, 130, 142

Queen, see *Hoontkymiha*
ranger, 1, 3-4, 29, 33, 37, 40-41, 46, 69, 90, 108, 124-125
red, 36, 54-55, 59, 61-66, 142, see vermillion
reservation, 23, 114

Sachem, vii, 5, 8
Saponi, ii-iii, 118
Saponie, ii, vi-vii, x, xii-xv, 2, 4, 6, 8-15, 17, 19-23, 25, 30-34, 37-42, 45-46, 48, 50-53, 55, 58-61, 63-66, 72, 75, 77-78, 81-82, 84-90, 94-98, 100-118, 120-124, 126, 129, 132-134, see also Sappone and Sappony
Saponie town, x, 32, 46 n.2, 47, 49-50, 52-53, 60-61, 77, 89-90, 129
Sappone cabins, 108
Sappony, ii, iv, 22, 58-59, 118, see also Saponie
Saraw, xii, 105-107

Scalps and scalping, 7, 58-59, 63, 85, 96, 98
Seneca, 4, 33, 96, 114
Shakori, 1
shot, *see* powder
slaves and slaving, xiii, 16, 30, 40, 68-70, 122-126, 129
spitting, 12-13
Spotswood, viii, ix-xi, xvi, 2-5, 9-10, 12, 15-22, 25-29, 31-35, 37, 39-41, 43, 46, 50, 67, 70-74, 77-78, 80, 82, 88-90, 92-93, 95-96, 98, 102-103, 110, 112-114, 116, 121, 124, 128
Stevenson, Christopher, iv, 109
sweating houses, 48

tattoos, 56-57, 63
Tottero, vi, xii, xiii*n*.6, 2, 17, 19, 22, 25, 31, 33, 46, 100-101, 107, 112-113, 115, 121, *see also* Tutelo
trade or traders, ix, xiii-xiv, 2-3, 9, 16-17, 21, 23, 28, 30-31, 33-40, 48, 57, 60-62, 64, 69, 71-75, 82-83, 88-89, 92-95, 98, 100-110, 120, 122, 126, 128-131, 133
Treaty of Middle Plantation (1677), 17-18, 20-21, 30, 45, 64, 132
Tributary Tribes, ii, vi, 18-23, 29-33, 35, 39-40, 45-46, 53, 55, 64-65, 67, 71-77, 80-84, 88, 94-102, 104, 106-107, 111-117, 120, 126, 132-133
Tuscarora, 16-17, 66, 74, 95-97, 101, 108, 114, 117, 132
Tutelo, 114-115, 118, *see also* Tottero
Tutelo-Saponi language, 118

vermillion, 36, 55-56, 61-64, 66, 142, *see* red

Wiccocomico, 23
woman, vii, 3, 19, 48, 121-126
women, xi-xii, xiv, 1, 7, 38, 56, 60-61, 64, 69, 82-83, 90-91, 97, 119-123, 126, 130-131

Yamasee, 16

www.ingramcontent.com/pod-product-compliance
Lightning Source LLC
Chambersburg PA
CBHW032053090426
42744CB00005B/203